KENGO KUMA *Point Line Plane*

KENGO KUMA *Point Line Plane*

With 72 illustrations

CONTENTS

A DISCOURSE ON METHOD

POINT

LINE

PLANE

FOREWORD

In 2004 I wrote a book called *Architecture of Defeat*, as a summary and critique of the 20th century. The 20th century was a period of 'victorious architecture' – buildings that employed the hard, strong, heavy material of concrete as a means of defeating the environment. As an alternative, I proposed the concept of 'defeated architecture'.

Although I was convinced that architecture of this kind would meet with a crushing defeat, I subsequently received a host of questions from people asking how it could best be defeated.

The book was not intended as an ideological sermon calling for the failure of architecture. When I began the book, I strove to deal with the subject matter in a realistic way, but while I was writing it became clear that unless I went way back in history – long before the 20th century – I would never find any method of defeat.

In more precise terms, the works of the early Italian Renaissance architects Alberti and Brunelleschi[1] proved to be a watershed in the development of a method of victory and defeat.

Although these units that make up architecture may have been small, they served as the basis for this method. At the same time, I realized that it was not enough to simply say that they were small. There are many kinds of smallness – for example, points, lines and planes. While a diverse range of small things might be embedded in each other and cause each other to jump, this might also amount to a vigorous 'failure'.

1 View of Florence cathedral Santa Maria del Fiore, dome designed by Brunelleschi

As I observed this state in which a dimension was embedded and began to jump, I realized that it was impossible to explain dimensional dislocation without addressing the question of time. Moreover, I realized that I had to bring human beings down to the same level as these small things. It was not so much that architecture had won, but that, by assuming a higher position, human beings had made and used architecture that had won.

I had been considering democratic and socially open architecture for many years, but now I had a hunch that this method could also be used to discuss and make things that were democratic. Thinking that this would lead to a variety of explorations regarding the method, I came to refer to this undertaking as a 'discourse on method'. This notion was supported by my own personal preferences, as I felt compelled to create physically large architecture. This made me wonder if it might be possible to create something that, while being large, existed in a small state that would convey a sense of defeat to people.

It was this sense of pressure that drove me to write this book.

9

A DISCOURSE ON METHOD

THE 20TH CENTURY: AN AGE OF VOLUME

I have recently come to see what I do as an effort to dismantle volume. By dismantling volume into points, lines and planes I am trying to let some fresh air inside. By letting fresh air inside, I am trying to reconnect people with things, the environment and each other.

Volume is a fundamental property of concrete architecture. The material is made by mixing gravel and sand with cement and water, which is allowed to dry and harden, creating volume from the outset. Conversely, points, lines and planes have a loose, fresh feeling that rejects mass (or volume).

I have spent many years considering my lifelong theme of moving from concrete to wood. Simply put, the 20th century was an age of concrete, with roots in an industrial society, but in today's post-industrial society it should be possible to make a variety of things out of wood, and to create a society that is symbolized by wood.

This is both my prediction and my hope. It is also for this reason that I created the new National Stadium for the 2020 Tokyo Olympics and Paralympics[2] by gathering timber from all over the country and using these small pieces of wood to assemble the structure by hand. This was intended to create a contrast with Kenzō Tange's Yoyogi National Gymnasium, designed for the 1964 Tokyo Olympics, which overwhelmed people with the structural beauty of the concrete.

As I was using wood, I did my best to avoid a closed volume and tried to create something with the looseness and openness that is characteristic of wood. The exterior

2 The new 2020 Olympic stadium in Tokyo. Japan.

of the stadium is covered completely with small point-like pieces of cedar only 10 cm (4 in.) wide, and thin line-like boards. Although the entire structure is large, what we see in front of us is a collection of small points and lines.

When you visit a building site it becomes abundantly clear that concrete is well suited to making a large mass. All you have to do is produce a mould and pour the slushy concrete into it, and you immediately end up with a closed volume. By contrast, steel and wood are like thin rods, which make it extremely laborious to create a volume; you have to firmly connect the rods and carefully fill the gaps between them.

Cramming as many people as possible into a large, robust volume made out of concrete formed the basis of the 20th-century lifestyle and economy, while the invention of air conditioning created the illusion that people were lucky to live in these unnaturally closed spaces. Prior to this, happiness could be found outside the volume – walking through an alley or lazing around on a veranda – but 20th-century people discarded these enjoyable and pleasant things and shut themselves inside, in the mistaken belief that they were happy.

The 20th century was an era in which enlarging a volume was seen as the ultimate goal. The housing shortage caused by the population explosion that followed World War II created the need for a huge number of houses, and there was also a massive demand for office space in city centres. The 20th century therefore demanded the speedy construction of building spaces with large volumes: corporations took pride in having large offices, and having a house with a large volume was seen as the height of human happiness. Not only was concrete well suited to volumes, it was quick to use, making it the perfect material for this slipshod era.

This also led to architecture becoming something that could be privately bought and sold, leading to its commodification. Something with an ambiguous link to its surroundings that could not be completely commoditized was difficult to price, or to buy and sell; fog and mist cannot be sold, for example. Clearly, detaching something from its environmental surroundings and turning it into a closed volume was a necessary requirement for a product. Lacking ambiguity, concrete was the ideal material for commercializing architecture and establishing private property. In this way, the 20th century became the era of concrete.

LINES IN JAPANESE ARCHITECTURE AND THE WORK OF MIES VAN DER ROHE

If concrete is well suited to the creation of three-dimensional volumes, Japanese wooden buildings are an architecture of lines; in other words, they are one-dimensional. By assembling (one-dimensional) linear timber that was easy to remove from the forest, filling in the gaps with mud walls and inserting lightweight furnishings such as *shoji* and *fusuma*, Japanese people created transparent and flexible spaces.[3]

Making something of this kind was far more labour intensive than using concrete, because it was extremely difficult to seal the gaps between the lines. Strictly speaking, Japanese wooden buildings are not completely sealed; they are made up of loose lines floating in the air, which improves ventilation and makes them physically comfortable. Generally, Japanese people did not care for the idea of being closed up in a concrete volume. In fact, when I go inside a concrete box, I feel suffocated. My body rejects concrete.

On the other hand, when Le Corbusier (1887–1965) was taken to Katsura Imperial Villa during a visit to Japan, he was repulsed by the building. A leading figure in 20th-century architectural design and a champion of concrete, he reportedly muttered: 'Too many lines.' From Le Corbusier's viewpoint – as the King of Concrete and a Volumist – the villa, with its beautiful balance of lines and planes, looked like a work of complicated architecture.

Another champion of 20th-century architecture, Mies van der Rohe (1886–1969), ranked with Le Corbusier but was distinctly different from him. He was a linear architect,

3 Gepparo teahouse. Katsura Imperial Villa. Kyoto. Japan. Traditional chaya (teahouse) built in the Edo period. 17th century.

who combined thin lines of metal sashes with planes of glass to create the prototype for the glass-clad high-rise building.

To make a high rise that repeats simple forms, it is possible to prepare the lines (steel and sashes) and the planes (glass and floorboards) beforehand at a factory and assemble them on site. This is infinitely easier than making a building by pouring concrete on site, and also speedier, yet still capable of creating large volumes. Mies realized this very early on, becoming a champion of 20th-century architecture that extolled compositions made up of lines and planes. In fact, high-rise buildings are still made by combining lines and planes, as people continue to copy Mies's original invention.

Personally, I do not find the spaces that Mies made to be comfortable. Although lines play a leading role in his work, his top priority was to effectively close the space, so the joy of freely floating points, lines and planes, and the transparency that you find in traditional Japanese architecture are nowhere to found. For Mies, closure was a categorical imperative, but being inside a glass-clad high rise equipped with good air conditioning can feel as if you are in a prison.

Part of the problem is that when you make a building out of glass, you do not end up with something transparent. Colin Rowe (1920–1999), an architectural historian who set out to establish Modernism as a leading force in the late 20th century, played an important role in architectural history as a whole. Rowe distinguished between 'literal' and 'phenomenal' transparency, warning against the supremacy of glass in the 20th century. He referred to the pursuit of plain and simple transparency that was achieved automatically by using glass as 'literal', while the technique of using a layered spatial structure (even without glass) to imply a space that was not actually visible in the background was described as 'phenomenal' transparency. As an example of the latter, Rowe cited the facade of San Giorgio Maggiore, which was designed by the Italian Mannerist architect Andrea Palladio (1508–1580), well before glass came into widespread use. He admired Palladio's work for both its depth and its refined, intellectual spatial structures.

However, when it comes to phenomenal transparency, nothing comes close to pre-Meiji Japanese wooden architecture, which was entirely free of glass. Palladio's work is no match for this multi-layered spatial structure (recalling a 12-layered ceremonial kimono) or the transparency produced by a combination of movable fixtures such as *shoji* and *fusuma*. Yet, Rowe makes no mention of Japan. He lived in an age of concrete, steel and glass, and traditional Japanese architecture – which lay outside these limitations – never entered his field of vision. Even an outstanding historian such as Rowe was only able to conceive of architecture within the material confines of the 20th century.

FROM KANDINSKY'S COMPOSITIONS
TO GIBSON'S PARTICLES

How might we free ourselves from the century of volume?
Is it possible to break the restraints of volume and recommit
our bodies to the free flow of matter and space? Thinking
that points, lines and planes might provide some hints,
I examined their potential in greater depth, and searched
for a method of dismantling volume. But before dealing
with the three elements individually, I reread *Point and Line
to Plane*, Wassily Kandinsky's[4] unforgettable 1926 book.

In 1922, the Bauhaus invited Kandinsky (1866–1944) to
teach at the integrated design institute, with the expecta-
tion that he would play a leading role at the cutting-edge
school. Today, at a time when the vertical divide between
the disciplines of art, architecture and design is seen as a
given, the Bauhaus education method seems amazingly
multidisciplinary. Kandinsky was particularly taken with
the school's fervour for tearing down the walls between
disciplines, and *Point and Line to Plane* is a collection of
legendary lectures that he gave at the Bauhaus.

I bought the book when I was in high school after being
intuitively drawn to its title. At the time, I was especially
interested in painting, but there were very few scientific
discussions or other texts on the subject. I was dissatisfied
with the objective, sentimental tone of painting treatises,
and was attracted instead to Kandinsky's matter-of-fact
mathematical typology of points, lines and planes.

That is not to say that I was completely won over by the
book. I remember feeling bewildered by the fact that it was

4 Wassily Kandinsky.
*Painting with Green
Center*. 1913. Oil on canvas.
108.9 × 118.4 cm
42 ⁷/₈ × 46 ⁵/₈ in.

a mixture of deeply interesting and deeply boring passages, and after rereading the book, it was abundantly clear to me which was which.

I grew irritated with the sections on Constructivism, and the parts in which Kandinsky analyses compositions made up of the three elements of points, lines and planes were especially tedious. I became fed up with the endless explanations in which he enumerated, classified and analysed the psychological effects of compositional techniques. In lengthy, detailed analyses that dealt with the relationship between compositions and their psychological effects, Kandinsky explained how configuring points and lines in a certain way creates a cold impression, while combining them in a different way makes them warm. But I lost interest completely. I came away with the feeling that regardless of the composition – whether you placed something on the right or left, or made something bigger or small – it would have very little effect psychologically. It seemed to me that other things drive the psyche.

In the early 20th century there was a boom in scientifically analysing the relationship between form and the psyche, leading to the emergence of phenomenology. Kandinsky's Constructivist analyses in *Point and Line to Plane* are part of the same tendency. This type of phenomenology strove to be a science, but it ultimately petered out without developing any concrete methodology.

The emergence of James J. Gibson's (1904–1979) Affordance Theory marked the end of this type of pseudo-scientific approach, which had come to seem very dated. In books such as *The Perception of the Visual World* (1950) and *The Senses Considered as Perpetual Systems* (1966), Gibson proclaimed the death of phenomenology. He rejected the concept of composition, choosing instead to address the question of texture. Based on a thorough empirical analysis, he concluded that the psychology and behaviour of living things was not determined by the composition of an environment, but rather by its textures. Gibson argued that by perceiving the environment as textures rather than a composition made up of points, lines and planes, it was possible to scientifically penetrate the relationship between the world and living things, and the environment and psychology.

GIBSON AND PARTICLES

One could say that Gibson liberated the world from being a continuum of three-dimensional volumes. He redefined the world not as a series of volumes, but as an aggregation of textures created by an agglomeration of countless dots and lines.

Part of the reason he was able to do this was that while he started out as a psychologist, he felt dissatisfied with the vagueness of the field and ventured into biology, endeavouring to grasp the realities of how living things perceive their environments based on the actualities of their bodies. He even delved into the structures of organisms' retinas, taking a scientific approach to something as seemingly indefinable as texture.

Another decisive experience for Gibson was his service in the Air Force during World War II, during which he was involved in the selection and training of pilots. By studying how pilots' bodies – moving at high speed in three dimensions – perceive space and distance, Gibson determined scientific formulae that showed how the body relates to space, discovering that pilots utilize texture to gauge distance and speed.

Gibson's revelations regarding texture caused me to see points, lines and planes in a radically different manner to the conventional Constructivist approach, and led me to believe that the environment is not composed of points, lines and planes, but textures that points, lines and planes generate.

Gibson focused firstly on how people gauge the depths of spaces and the distances of objects. The prevailing wisdom

5 White Cube Bermondsey. London.
United Kingdom.

was that people estimate distance and depth using stereoscopic vision, based on the parallax between the left and
right eyes. However, stereoscopic vision does not work in
this way for pilots moving at extremely high speeds.

In general, people use elements such as points and lines
to measure the depths of spaces; to gauge the speed of their
own movement; and to assess how far away objects are. The
absence of such particles (or elements) as points and lines
leads to anxiety, and human beings – indeed, organisms of
all kinds – cannot inhabit such a world.

The modern architecture that emerged at the start of the
20th century did not acknowledge the value of particles,
and was oriented towards colourless, abstract spaces that
were often described as 'white cubes'.[5] If forced to fend for
itself in such a space, no organism could survive for long.
However, while modern architecture aspired to empty

6 Pablo Picasso. *Les Demoiselles d'Avignon.* 1907. Oil on canvas. 240 230 cm 94 ½ 90 ½ in.

white space, particles such as furniture, lighting fixtures and accessories were distributed throughout these spaces, enabling human beings to adapt to the environment.

INTELLECTUALISM VS DADA

After encountering Gibson, I felt I understood the reasons for my scepticism towards Constructivism in art. It is said that in the early years of the 20th century, art experienced two revolutions: Cubism, a revolution of form, and Fauvism, a revolution of colour.

These two revolutions ostensibly shattered all the rules established previously, and gave artists total freedom. However, after the Cubist revolution, its standard-bearers, Pablo Picasso[6] (1881–1973) and Georges Braque (1882–1963), continued to work figuratively, rather than turning towards abstraction. Both Picasso and Braque sensed the chaos and futility that could ensue as soon as the constraint of rendering specific objects was removed.

Every revolution is followed immediately by the onset of intellectual arrogance in the form of structure and organization. Whether the revolution is artistic or political, the victors in the revolutionary conflict – the newly crowned elite – will seek to rule the world through organization, or planning, by actors with agency and privilege who view things from a meta-level. In politics and economics, intellectualism takes the form of planning. A prime example can be seen in the USSR, which was an experiment with a centralized planned economy; a petri dish for the chaos and futility of 'planning'.

Recognizing the futility of the 'top-down' approach – organization and planning, or Constructivism in art – Picasso and others adhered to figuration. Meanwhile, at the same time as Constructivism, another art movement known as Dada emerged. Dada has been perceived as a nihilistic movement that served as a critical and destructive reaction to the tradition and convention rooted in a sense of emptiness and absurdity following the horrors of World War I.

However, the essence of Dada lay in opposition to intellectualism and Constructivism. Dada's emphasis on chance critiqued the actions of the powers that be, which take a bird's-eye view of the whole and intellectually construct and plan subordinate parts. The Dadaists' reverence for unplanned chance was not at all destructive, but rather a manifestation of respect for natural, free-flowing time. It was not nihilism, but a sincere response to the materials and intervals of time at hand, based on a ground-level perspective. For this reason the Dadaists had strong affection for everyday objects and craftsmanship, and showed interest in performing and media arts such as dance and film, which are often regarded as inferior to fine art. My scepticism towards Constructivism – the discussion of which occupies around half of Kandinsky's *Point and Line to Plane* – and affinity for Dada reflected my sympathies with the ground-level physicality of the Dada perspective.

That said, while rereading Kandinsky I found he made many novel points that transcended Constructivism or intellectualism. For example, he noted that the classification of points, lines and planes is inherently relative and can never be absolute; what one believes to be a point could suddenly reveal itself as a line or a plane, and what appears to be a plane could manifest as a point.

For Kandinsky, classifications such as architecture, painting and music were also fluid. He rejected the categorization of artistic disciplines outright, stating that they were all embedded in one another. In one half of *Point and Line to Plane* he freely traverses the conventional boundaries imposed on the vertically divided world, and his discussion tramples through the fields of human creative endeavour like a wild horse galloping across the heavens.

The Bauhaus – the ground-breaking educational institution that was ground zero for such erasure of boundaries (between artistic disciplines, or between fine and applied arts) – also had close ties to Dada, that movement often dismissed as destructive or nihilistic.

The Bauhaus originated in 1919 in Weimar, Germany, and the city became the centre of Dada after the members left the movement's birthplace of Zürich, Switzerland. In Weimar, the Dadaists spent their days drinking and immersing themselves in atonal music, and one could say that the proximity of Dada helped give the Bauhaus license to shatter boundaries. Indeed, the architect Theo van Doesburg (1883–1931), who taught at the Bauhaus, was strongly connected to Dada. Speaking of 'infusing the poison of the new spirit everywhere', he adopted a rebellious stance that seemed out of place at the Bauhaus, the high temple of functionalism.

FROM TIME AS MOTION TO TIME AS MATERIAL

Kandinsky called the belief that painting is an art of space and music is an art of time no more than a mass delusion, and asserted that by applying the vocabulary of points (or musical notes), lines and planes to both, the experiences of these art forms could be analysed scientifically on the same level.

Kandinsky was not the first person to note affinities between music and architecture. In the earliest known example, the philosopher Friedrich Schelling (1775–1854), one of the best-known thinkers in the German idealist movement, defined architecture as 'music in space', and Johann Wilhelm von Goethe (1749–1832) commented that 'architecture is frozen music'.

In Japan, it is well known that Ernest Fenollosa (1853–1908) described the east pagoda of Yakushi-ji Temple as 'frozen music'. Fenollosa is known as one of the first Westerners to appreciate Japanese art, but he was also well versed in music, as his father was a Spanish musician who travelled to the United States on a frigate as a shipboard pianist.

These poetic words from long ago may seem to point to affinities between architecture and music, but to me it sounds as if they underscore the contrast between the two,

7 Wassily Kandinsky. *Violett.*
1923. Lithograph in red. yellow.
blue and black. 29.1 19.1 cm
11 ½ 7 ½ in.

as in fact music flows by and disappears over time, while
architecture is frozen, fixed in place and unable to flow away.

Kandinsky, however, thought of architecture as a fluid
and phenomenological entity that was not at all stationary,
and believed there was no fundamental difference between
music and architecture. The discovery of a common concept
(point, line, plane) extending across disciplines led to
Kandinsky's denial of and boundaries between disciplines,
and point, line and plane became useful tools for breaking
down the walls that separated them.

Kandinsky's boundary-shattering analysis expanded
to printmaking[7] and to the issue of modifications made to
prints. To make such modifications is to amend what was
made in the past; it is an additive act on the axis of time.

By focusing on the act of modification, Kandinsky succeeded in inserting the element of time into the two-dimensional art form of printmaking. Time is said to be the fourth dimension, and here, Kandinsky superimposed that fourth dimension on printmaking, which is thought of as a two-dimensional art. The reader is astonished to find printmaking – considered a small and relatively minor sub-category of the two-dimensional arts – suddenly released by Kandinsky's discussion into the vastness of the temporal world and cosmos.

Specifically, by adding the axis of time, Kandinsky clarifies essential differences among copperplate printmaking, woodcuts and lithography (which was originally executed on stone plates). He described the three materials (copper, wood and stone) in terms of their relation to time: in copperplate printmaking it is basically impossible to make modifications after the fact; in woodcuts modifications are possible with limitations; and in lithography one is free to make modifications without limits. It was because he was an artist himself that Kandinsky was able to connect time and material in this way.

Many art critics view 'dead' (finished) works and discuss their compositions or the subjects and points in time depicted therein; for example, a painting in which it is twilight in autumn. However, for an artist, time is not something depicted in a work, rather the creation of the work is itself an intervention in time. In other words, the artist lives in the midst of the raw process of creation. Because Kandinsky was himself an artist, he was able to use printmaking – a small-scale two-dimensional medium – to describe how artists and time interact in various ways. For their makers, prints are not 'dead' works, but live on in the same time continuum as the artist.

As soon as Kandinsky focuses attention on the practicalities of printmaking and the grubby, earthbound matter of the material, it is linked to a formless, cosmic entity: time. The three media of copperplate printmaking, woodcuts and lithography are profoundly connected to the materials of copper, wood and stone, and each material is connected to time through its own distinctive procedure. In this way, Kandinsky informs us that there is material in time and time in material.

I had a strong sense that if this idea were to be applied to architectural design, it would open up unprecedented, ground-breaking perspectives, and the concept of time in architecture would emerge in completely new ways.

FROM ADDITIVE DESIGN TO COMPUTATIONAL DESIGN

The multi-layered concept of time that Kandinsky found in printmaking offers many suggestions for ways of thinking about new design methods in post-industrial society, such as computer-based parametric design. Since the early 1990s, the debate over how computers are changing design in architecture, and changing the relationships between people and architecture, has roiled the architectural world, and has become central to architectural theory.

The history of architecture has always been the creation of new designs using new technologies; from ancient times to the present, new technologies have opened up new architectural modalities. However, if the modern architecture of the 20th century was the product of new technologies that enabled large-span steel and concrete structures, what is the architectural product of today's computer technology?

The architectural historian, Mario Carpo (b. 1958), boldly addresses the issue by comparing computational design with various other design methods from the Renaissance onwards, and sees computational design as radically transforming architecture from subtractive to additive design.

In *The Alphabet and the Algorithm* (2011), Carpo notes that computational design has not only changed the way blueprints (drawings) are rendered, but has also facilitated the integration of drawing and fabrication. Carpo recognizes that whereas the production of drawings and the construction of buildings were previously disconnected, computers have transformed the process so that the two form a continuous, seamless flow. Architecture no longer consists of self-contained works, but has become an on-going system that is continually changed and modified, which he calls 'additive design'.

Just as Kandinsky noted that a lithograph is infinitely modifiable and can always be added to, Carpo notes that the computer has made endless addition possible. To pursue the metaphor, the computer has transformed architecture from a scarcely modifiable 'woodcut' system to an ever-changing 'lithographic' system.

In Carpo's analysis, architecture was similarly additive prior to the Renaissance, when clients, construction foremen and labourers worked together, continually creating and renovating the loosely defined structures that made up architecture. This changed when Leon Battista Alberti (1404–1472) stepped into this laid-back world and radically changed the way the discipline was practised.

Alberti was one of the leading architects and architectural theorists of the early Renaissance, who introduced the subtractive method and the idea of the 'creator' as an absolute authority who does not permit changes or modifications after construction is complete.

Carpo points out that this shift resulted in a loss of the freedom originally inherent to architecture, making it a rigid, inflexible system that only gives solid form to the drawings of the architect; the absolute authority. In Carpo's view, the computer broke the shackles that had endured over the centuries that followed Alberti. Before Alberti there was no sharp division, and no conflict, between the architect (maker of drawings) and the artisan (maker of buildings), but rather a slow, continuous process of creation and change. Carpo's prediction is that computer fabrication will revive the intense bonds and sense of unity between people and things that once existed.

At the same time, Carpo notes that the introduction of computers to the architectural field did not originally have an additive intent. Computers were introduced and the term 'parametric design' came into use in the early 1990s, but computers were merely machines used to create soft and innovative forms. Before then, drawing complex forms was incredibly time-consuming, so the computer was adopted initially as a convenient device that could realize the forms of architects' dreams. Carpo harshly criticized this form of computational design, as merely a 1990s update of the flowing, streamlined look and eccentric forms[8] that were popular in the US in the 1930s.

However, towards the middle of the 1990s, computational design entered a second phase, which saw the focus shift from novelty of form to fabrication processes. The boundary between drawing and building faded, and interest shifted to architecture that continued to change, even after construction was completed. Carpo calls this the second era of digital design.

Underlying Carpo's two-stage theory is the classic
book, *Theory & Design in the First Machine Age* (1960), by
the architectural historian Reyner Banham (1922–1988).
Banham summarized relationships between humans and
machines in the 19th and 20th centuries, and asserted that
there was a qualitative difference between the first generation of machines, such as steam engines and automobiles,
and the second generation, which includes radios, televi-
sions and household appliances. Banham concluded that
this difference had a significant impact on the architectural
design of the time and, taking his cue from this, Carpo
determined that the age of computers has already had
two stages thus far.

Once set, concrete is hard and dense, and does not allow for unlimited modifications. This makes it thoroughly unsuitable for the second phase of computational design: enabling the eternal modifications demanded by the age of additive design. Concrete lost its central position in architectural design, and structures were increasingly created through the aggregation of small units. As a prominent practitioner of this new wave of modular architecture, I felt encouraged by Carpo's arguments.

An interesting point that can be made here is that computational design was not a revolution of form, but rather of time. The idea that form reigns supreme is a product of modernity going back to Alberti, but today, a paradigm shift from design based on form to design based on time is underway. It can be said that Carpo's discussion of time-based design theory had already been anticipated by Kandinsky's discussion of printmaking.

BRUNO LATOUR AND THE CHRONOPHOTOGRAPHIC GUN

In the past, I have discussed the idea that our approach to design is additive with the French anthropologist and philosopher Bruno Latour (1947–2022). Latour is known as a proponent of a new world view known as ANT (Actor–Network Theory), which builds on the work of post-structuralist thinkers of the preceding generation, including Michel Foucault (1926–1984), Jacques Derrida (1930–2004) and Gilles Deleuze (1925–1995). According to Latour, this preceding generation had endeavoured to dismantle the subject (as in subject vs object), but had been unable to break free of basic tenets of Western philosophy, notably anthropocentrism. This was because no matter how they might critique the privilege and complacency of the subject, they remained solely focused on human beings.

Latour holds that human beings living alongside and collaborating with various other entities make the world go round. He calls these entities 'actors'. The crux of ANT is that there is no hierarchy of human and non-human, and that all are actors working in concert. For example, Latour points out that when we attempt to shape a material using a tool, we are not in a superior position to the material or the tool; we are not only utilizing these things, but also learning and receiving instructions from them.

My interaction with Latour began when one of his pupils, Sophie Houdart (b. 1971), came to my office to study my architectural design process, and offered to write a book on the subject. Latour had previously researched the methods employed by the office of Rem Koolhaas (b. 1944), and with his pupil, Albena Yaneva, co-wrote the book *Give Me a Gun and I Will Make All Buildings Move: An ANT's View of Architecture* (2008). Here, ANT stands for 'Actor–Network Theory', but it is also a pun on 'ant' (the insect). The book's intent is to view the architectural process through the eyes of an ant; from a terrestrial or microscopic perspective rather than a macroscopic or bird's-eye view.

In critiques of architecture, philosophers of the post-structuralist generation focused on the massive, static and dull nature of buildings, with the volumes of huge, immovable structures designed by those with privilege and agency coming into their crosshairs. However, Latour and his colleagues stated that a building from an ant's perspective it is not at all static, and the eyes of the ant can be contrasted with the chronophotographic gun invented by the French physiologist Etienne-Jules Marey (1830–1904).

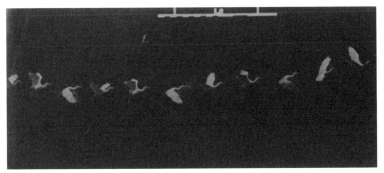

9 Etienne-Jules Marey. *Chronophotograph of a Flying Heron.* c. 1883–87.
Gelatin silver print. 8.3 × 9.4 cm 3 ¼ × 3 ¾ in.

With this device, things that appear to be in motion
abruptly become a sequence of freeze-frame images.[9] The
ant's eye, on the contrary, is a means of dramatically redis-
covering apparently stationary buildings as constantly
moving and changing. This is the source of *Give Me a Gun*.

Houdart visited our office repeatedly over the course
of a year and observed the actual design process with the
closeness and continuity of an ant, compiling the results in a
book entitled *Kuma Kengo: An Unconventional Monograph*
(2009). From this ant's-eye view, she reported on the state
of our office, in which inanimate objects such as models,
samples and CAD, and human actors such as the staff,
outsourced engineers, subcontractors and construction
contractors, form a close network like ants.

She also observed how buildings are designed, constructed and continue to change, even after completion.
The structures we create are not stationary in the least,
and Houdart recognized that our architecture is a space
to which various things continue to be added, and in which
small particles are continually flowing. For me, working
with Latour and Houdart opened up new vistas revealing
relationships between time and architecture, and networks
that link people, objects and buildings.

ARCHITECTURE AND TIME

The connection between time and space is a fascinating theme that has been discussed repeatedly in traditional architectural theory. A classic example is *Space, Time and Architecture* (1941) by Sigfried Giedion (1888–1968), a Swiss architectural historian who witnessed the birth of 20th-century modernism around the same time as Kandinsky. On publication, Giedion's book was highly lauded and even called 'the Bible of modern architecture', although one would now have to say that Giedion was overrated due to the concept of space and time being so dominant in the arts in the early 20th century.

The stimulus for this craze came from Albert Einstein (1879–1955). Following Einstein's completion of his theory of relativity in physics, painting movements such as Cubism and Surrealism emerged that endeavoured to integrate multiple points in time on a single picture plane. In architecture, Le Corbusier inserted an observer's pathway through the built space at the centre of his master-work, Villa Savoye (1931),[10] calling it 'the Architectural Promenade' and describing it as a model of the integration of space and time. In an amusing illustration of the extent of Einstein's influence (not only in science, but also in the art world at the time) Le Corbusier went so far as to invite Einstein to the Villa Savoye and give him a personal tour.

Giedion expanded on this idea, announcing to the world that modern architecture had achieved the fusion of time and space. He cleverly constructed his argument as if Einsteinian physics underpinned modern architecture,

but his logic was facile. The notion is that utilizing elements that enable movement – such as ramps and stairs – as the centrepieces in the atrium space, as in Villa Savoye, constitutes a fusion of time and space. But this is not a new argument. Giedion simply applied to architecture the theory behind Marcel Duchamp's Cubist painting, *Nude Descending a Staircase No. 2*, 1912, namely that time and space can be linked by superimposing people and objects in motion on a single picture plane.

Seen another way, the fact that discussions of this nature were so popular in the early 20th century illustrates the extent of popular enthusiasm for motion at the time. Both artists and the general public were overwhelmed by the advent of automobiles and airplanes, and by the way people were moving at speeds they had never experienced before.

Time was equated with objects in motion, leaving no room for thinking about other aspects or manifestations of time. Compared to this 'motion = time' paradigm that dominated the early 20th century, Kandinsky's perspective is highly original; its scope extends well beyond shallow fads inspired by automobiles and airplanes, remaining relevant today.

LIBERATING TIME FROM MOTION

It is possible to summarize Wassily Kandinsky's achievement as the liberation of time from motion. As a result of listening closely to dialogues between materials and time at sites of production, time revealed itself to him in unexpected ways.

I have the ambition to do something similar. Is it possible to weave a new theory of time from the threads of my day-to-day life, in which I continually converse with various materials, observing how materials flow in time and how time affects materials? To me, time is not mere motion, but something fundamentally embedded in all matter; and through matter, space and time are inseparably connected. Specific materials, such as wood and stone, make their way through space as a function of time. This may seem like a trivial discovery, but it may actually be a great revelation with vast cosmic scope.

Le Corbusier, on the other hand, didn't connect material and time. For him, materials were no more than stagehands assisting in the production of the main attraction: the abstract white cube. He believed that if you created a white cube that induced motion, objects would move around inside that white cube according to the laws of motion. Like many of his contemporaries, he believed

11 Terrace and ramp to the second floor at the Villa Savoye at Poissy. France.

that motion was the essence of time; even the ramp going through the centre of Villa Savoye[11] was a blank white background, intended to present motion symbolically.

The perception of time embodied by Villa Savoye is that of Isaac Newton (1642–1727), who made the world-changing discovery that the movement of objects in abstract spaces is governed by laws of motion. That was centuries before Albert Einstein, and neither Le Corbusier nor the rest of the modernist architects had caught up to Einstein (who had rejected Newton's model), and certainly never extended to the post-Einsteinian world of quantum mechanics.

However, to give Le Corbusier his due, I should specify that Villa Savoye is a classic example of early Le Corbusier. In Le Corbusier's later works, such as Sainte Marie de La Tourette (1957) and Notre-Dame du Haut (1955), abstract, empty white space is no longer the goal. With its coarse and uneven textures, the concrete in late Le Corbusier is not merely a backdrop, but a conscious material that speaks and is aware of itself. It is a material that continues to weather and deteriorate over time; a deep, rich substance that is intimately wedded to time and has both past and future embedded within it.

I believe it was Le Corbusier's encounter with India that led him to this changed view of materials. Starting in 1951, Le Corbusier was involved in the urban planning of the Indian city of Chandigarh, and with the red soil of India he encountered a new variety of concrete with a new kind of materiality. It was concrete unlike any he had ever known: rough, uneven and unsanitary concrete that refused to obey orders. Through this encounter he must have also recognized that time is embedded in materials, and I am grateful to Le Corbusier's work in India for inspiring the new architecture I am seeking, and the relationship between architecture and time.

KANDINSKY'S TRANSCENDENCE AND EMBEDDING OF DIMENSIONS

Long before Le Corbusier's encounter with India, Kandinsky sought to remove the boundaries between time, matter and space. He was also endeavouring to erase the boundaries between the categories of point, line, plane and volume. In his book he examines the world in chapters dedicated to points, lines and planes, while at the same time declaring the four categories (those three, plus volumes) invalid.

What was most novel to me in this book was Kandinsky's assertion that the Gothic architecture of medieval Europe – which I had only ever seen as consisting of volumes – was actually an 'architecture of points'. Speaking in auditory

12 Unite d'Habitation in south
Marseille. France.

terms, Kandinsky describes the timbre of the Gothic as
brisk, crisp and sharply resonant. It represents a moment of
transition, when spatial forms dissolve into the atmosphere
around the structure and their sound fades away.

Similarly, Kandinsky notes that the distinctive Chinese
soaring roof also consists of points on the verge of disap-
pearing into thin air, providing an excellent answer to my
question as to why Qing Dynasty (1636–1912) Chinese
buildings favoured such exaggerated, even unnatural
concave curvature. Qing Dynasty rooflines taper radically
upwards in an attempt to melt into the air. In this sense,
the roofs of the Qing Dynasty share the same drive toward
levitation as the piloti of Le Corbusier.[12]

Underlying Kandinsky's analysis is a rejection of the
conventional framework of dimensions (the first, second,

third and fourth dimensions, or points, lines, planes and time). It thoroughly shatters our understanding of the world through the lens of dimensions, in the same way our understanding has been shattered by quantum mechanics. Just as Le Corbusier and Sigfried Giedion sought to keep company with Einstein, I too have turned to new advances in physics for guidance, and have found an abundance of freely available tools for understanding the world. With these tools, is it possible to punch holes in the paradigm of modernist architecture based on Newtonian mechanics' world view?

One of the greatest challenges of quantum mechanics is the presence of multiple spatial dimensions beyond the third. Quantum mechanics asserts that all manner of phenomena in our universe are inexplicable without positing these multiple dimensions, which cannot be imagined with our everyday senses. For example, it has been said that the cosmos cannot be explained unless we assume 10 dimensions: nine to define space, plus the dimension of time. But what on earth does it mean to state that there are six higher dimensions embedded in the cosmos, in addition to the three spatial dimensions we know of? How can we possibly comprehend a nine-dimensional space that transcends our ordinary powers of perception?

In his book, *What is Gravity*? (2012), Hirosi Ooguri (b. 1962), a prominent physicist in the field of particle theory, uses the metaphor of a hose and an ant to explain these higher dimensions in a straightforward manner:

'Think of an ant crawling on top of a hose used to water a garden. For the ant, the surface of the hose is a two-dimensional space on which it can move either vertically or horizontally. But… what if a bird flies down and perches on the hose? The bird's feet are wider than the hose is thick, so it can only move along the length of the hose… In other words, the hose, which is a two-dimensional space to the ant, is perceived as only a one-dimensional space by the bird. Only able to move vertically along the "one-dimensional" hose, the bird cannot sense the "higher dimension" of horizontality.'

NEW WORLD VIEWS AND
EFFECTIVE THEORIES

Ooguri brilliantly employs an everyday scene to explain how any number of dimensions might be embedded in space. Put another way, in the new model of dimensions presented by quantum physics, there are relative shifts in dimensions depending on the distance between the subject (the bird) and the object (the hose), and on differences in scale.

With reference to this relativistic world view, physics employs the term 'effective theory'. This refers to the idea that any theory is only effective within a framework at a given scale, and that all theories and laws are limited and relative, valid only at certain scales. Newton's law remains an effective theory in that it works perfectly well in the spaces immediately around us, at everyday scale and everyday speeds. The emergence of Einstein, or of quantum mechanics, does not mean that Newtonian mechanics has lost its validity at a given scale.

Quantum mechanics has done more than offer a new way of viewing the universe. I believe the greatest achievement of physics since the advent of quantum mechanics is that it has introduced a relativistic outlook, in which even quantum mechanics itself is only an effective theory.

For architects, a relativistic, 'effective theory-style' world view splendidly corresponds to and resonates with

13 The coexistence or ultra-large and ultra-small —
red-billed oxpeckers on a zebras back.

the current phenomena of dramatic expansion and diversification of scale that we are dealing with. We, too, grasp
the world 'effective theory style' as we carry out design. The
ability to observe both the world of subatomic particles and
the furthest reaches of the universe has qualitatively transformed physics, and a similar transformation is taking place
in the world of architecture. In this book I am looking for
new theoretical tools that can illuminate our environment,
in which the ultra-large and the ultra-small co-exist.[13]

AN EXPANDED. MULTI-LAYERED WORLD

Until the 19th century, it was the job of architects to
design medium-sized ('size M') buildings. Before steel and
concrete became the dominant building materials, there
were limits to the sizes of buildings that could be built.
These size limitations existed whether the material was
wood, stone or brick; there could be no architecture other
than size M architecture, which fell within those bounds.

14 Rembrandt van Rijn. *Landscape with Three Cottages along a Road.*
1650. Etching. 16.2   20.3 cm 6 ³⁄₈   8 in.

There is a reason for starting this discussion at size M
rather than size S (small). Size S refers to small folk dwellings and rural villages,[14] which predated the discipline of
architecture. Folk dwellings do not require the authoritative
designer known as an architect; it was only after architecture advanced to size M that architects and architectural
theory appeared.

From the Renaissance (Leon Battista Alberti) onwards,
architecture came to be seen as a central part of culture
along with painting, sculpture and music, but architectural
theory did not deal with size S structures, only size M. It is
safe to say that from the outset, Renaissance architects dis-
regarded the existence of folk dwellings and rural villages.

At size M, buildings were a collection of voids known as
rooms. Architectural design dealt with ways of arranging

and combining the rooms, and with varieties of silhouettes or external skins for the resulting structure.

The concept of size M architecture comes from Rem Koolhaas, in his book of essays on contemporary cities *S, M, L, XL* (1995). Before this book, amazingly, there had been no in-depth explorations of scale in the architectural world. This is because due to technological and economic constraints, size M remains the basic premise of architecture, and recent buildings of size L or XL have been an unexpected phenomenon. Size S is, as always, outside architects' field of vision.

Koolhaas is the first architect to think about what architecture might look like after the collapse of this basic premise, and I imagine that the catalyst for this shift in thinking may have come from his experiences in Asia, including Japan and China.

THE EXTRA LARGE ARCHITECTURE OF FINANCIAL CAPITALISM

Koolhaas first encountered Japan during the economic bubble era of the 1980s. He was invited during that unique time to work on projects so far-fetched that they could not have been imagined in Europe in that period. Swept by the sudden advent of full-fledged financial capitalism, Japan experienced economic growth at a scale and speed exceeding global norms at the time, and a large number of naïve 'dream projects' were launched, meeting with little or no resistance. Koolhaas was asked to work on several projects, including Kumamoto Artpolis and Nexus Housing Fukuoka, and got the sense that the era of size M

STAGES IN THE DESIGN FOR THE CHRYSLER BUILDING—FINAL STAGE IS SHOWN AT THE RIGHT—WILLIAM VAN ALEN, ARCHITECT
Materials are used in an interesting way in this building as follows: First story and entrances in black granite; second and third stories in Georgia marble; black, white, and gray brick above with some Georgia marble inlay, copings and entire top feature in Nirosta Steel; spandrels from 19th to 22nd stories in ornamental aluminum.

15 Stages in the design for the Chrysler Building. 1929.

architecture was ending and that of size L (large) and size XL (extra large) was beginning in Asia.

Koolhaas had long been interested in the new architecture of financial capitalism; if Le Corbusier was the champion of industrial-capitalist architecture, Koolhaas began his career aspiring to be a champion of financial capitalism. Seeking inspiration for post-capitalist architecture in grand buildings from the years just prior to the Great Depression – such as the Empire State Building (1930), the Chrysler Building (1928)[15] and the Downtown Athletic Club (1931) – he made a spectacular debut with his book *Delirious New York: A Retrospective Manifesto for Manhattan* (1978).

Zaha Hadid (1950–2016), a friend and former schoolmate of Koolhaas at the AA (Architectural Association School of Architecture) in London, was a founding member of OMA, the design firm Koolhaas launched. Like Koolhaas, she drew much inspiration from the pre-Depression architecture commonly known as Art Deco, and eventually became a diva of financial-capitalist architecture from the 1990s. She was also the winner of the first competition for the new Olympic stadium in Tokyo and when asked 'If you were to take one book with you to a desert island, what would it be?' Hadid replied that it would be *Delirious New York*. This response hints at both the bond between Hadid and Koolhaas, and the relationship of both to the world of finance.

That world of finance flowered briefly in 1920s New York, and as stock and real estate prices soared, architects revelled in megastructures with fantastic forms and outlandish programmes. However, these strange and beautiful blossoms were scattered by the stock market crash of 1929, which ushered in an era of solid, hardworking industrial capitalism, championed by the concrete-loving Le Corbusier and the steel-frame maestro Mies van der Rohe.

It was in the pre-Depression buildings Koolhaas discusses in *Delirious New York* that he found hints for the architecture of bubble-era Japan following the Plaza Accord (1985). Predicting that the static systems of industrial capitalism could no longer underpin a vast and ever-expanding world, he turned his eyes to the Roaring Twenties instead. Koolhaas and Hadid foresaw that digitization and the networking of national economies would leave the zombie-like resurrection of financial capitalism as the only means of supporting a growing world, and found an architectural style that was an optimum fit for financial capitalism. In doing so they became darlings of the financial sector; mad, gigantic projects in Japan during the bubble era, and later in China and other Asian countries, awakened Koolhaas and led him to write *S, M, L, XL*.

I, too, have had to consider the consequences of an expanding world governed by a rigidly hierarchical scale from S to XL. However, rather than taking a pessimistic and cynical view of the direction of this expanding world, as Koolhaas did, I am endeavouring to decipher it with reference to quantum mechanics and the idea of the effective theory. To prolong the life of our environment, what we need is not to laugh cynically at the collapse of the intellectualist approach, as Koolhaas has done – cynicism is a fruitless flight from reality. What we need is the flexibility of Dadaism, which flows along with the continuous currents of time and the material world.

THE EXPANSION OF ARCHITECTURE AND THE NEW PHYSICS

The development of Newtonian physics ran parallel to the transition from Renaissance-style size M architecture to Industrial Revolution-style size L architecture. In terms of historical causality, Newtonian physics triggered the Industrial Revolution, which in turn triggered the shift from size M architecture to size L. Concrete and steel boosted the maximum building size from size M to size L, producing large spaces with high ceilings and no columns, in buildings that had previously been no more than aggregations of small rooms.

The basis of Newton's physics is the movement of objects in abstract, empty space, governed by Newtonian equations. The way things people move about freely in large, abstract spaces, made possible by concrete and steel, reflects Newtonian physics perfectly. Le Corbusier designed the atrium of Villa Savoye to symbolize motion, but in retrospect this atrium was still bucolic size M architecture. With the new technologies of the early 20th century, such as elevators and escalators, empty spaces as containers for motion grew enormous, and the theoretical voids as containers of motion posited by Newtonian physics became a reality that spread across the world.

Just as the transition from Renaissance size M architecture to industrial size L architecture was not simply a matter of scale, so the transition from industrial-capitalist size L to financial-capitalist size XL was more than a change of scale; it represented a major qualitative shift in architecture and lifestyle.

For a start, the constraints posed by building site sizes were eliminated. In Japan, combining multiple plots of land and incorporating the interfering roads and rail lines that had run between them created huge new building sites. With massive developments such as Roppongi Hills and Tokyo Midtown,[16] which swallowed up small plots and narrow streets, size XL architecture and XL lifestyles emerged.

This was not merely a quantitative transition based on an increase in the area of building sites: the integration of sites signified the emergence of financial liquidity, as well as the emergence of political and economic coordination on an international scale. Without political and economic collusion across national borders, the unstable systems of financial capitalism could not be safely operated.

The post-industrial capitalist era has been just such an era of fluidity and collusion, and it is not the least bit coincidental that this transcendence of scale through fluidity took place in 'old-fashioned' Asia. Democratic systems built up in the West over many centuries only function to put

16 Aerial view of metropolitan Tokyo at dusk from atop the Mori Tower at Roppongi Hills. Tokyo. Japan.

the brakes on economic fluidity and the collusion between business and politics. As long as there is reverence for Western-style individualism, the transition from size M to size L is the most that can be achieved. Only in the context of Asian totalitarianism could size L projects swell across multiple sites, transgress established rules and laws, and make the jump to XL.

In physics, the analogue to this new XL paradigm is quantum mechanics, in that XL means not just colossal size, but the mixing and layering of numerous scales, from the microscopic to the vast. This multi-layering is the basic condition of XL. As such, melding and superimposition of a kind that had never occurred under Western-style democracy and rule of law emerged for the first time in the context of Asian totalitarianism.

Not only Newtonian physics, but even Einsteinian physics is incapable of explaining the chaotic situation that emerged with the rise of Asia. Einstein showed that space and time are one, and that at extremely high speeds both space and time expand and contract. He also proved brilliantly that the expansion and contraction of all space and time are governed by one beautiful equation: $E = mc^2$.

Although Einstein denied the existence of the conventional framework of space and time and shattered the barrier between these two worlds, he also stated that the new integrated world was still governed by laws. He did not reject the rule of law, so to speak, and in that sense Einstein could be called conservative.

However, current quantum mechanics has revealed that one law can no longer explain everything. It has become possible to make observations at the smallest and the largest scales, and we have learned that there is no law to rule it all. This can be equated with a denial of physics itself, as physics has traditionally been a discipline dedicated to searching for laws and uncovering equations. Einstein can be seen as the culmination – and the swan song – of that old physics.

By contrast, quantum mechanics rejects outright the scientific stance of calculating and predicting all things based on laws. Physics has lost its basic premise as an academic discipline, and the new, anarchic physics is a decisive departure from all physics up to Einstein.

FROM AN EVOLUTIONARY MODEL
TO A MULTI-LAYERED MODEL

What sort of new architecture will develop in parallel with the new physics, and what insights can the new architecture derive from the new physics?

The most intriguing aspect of the new physics is its departure from evolutionary logical structure, yet the logical structure of Rem Koolhaas's *S, M, L, XL* is essentially evolutionary and linear. It has a pessimistic vision rooted in the theory of evolution, in which small buildings have gradually grown and expanded to size M, then size L, and then exploded to size XL with the rise of Asia, plunging the world into an apocalypse of hopelessness.

This may seem to be a critique of the global status quo, but it is also an example of the European elite bemoaning the new state of Asia with all its turmoil and chaos. Koolhaas's generation has often criticized today's cities and architecture in this pessimistic sort of tone – a tone that fundamentally characterizes, for example, the urban and architectural thinking of Arata Isozaki (1931–2022). Their basic point is that as the world has gradually expanded, it has plummeted toward the brink of collapse, and there is no longer any hope of salvation. Meanwhile, the writer is a wise sage who alone sees the situation clearly, while deriding the rank-and-file architects swept along by this apocalyptic tide.

Writing in this mode may be just fine for architects of Isozaki's and Koolhaas's generation who encountered the XL paradigm later in life, but from the perspective of members of our generation, who started out as architects in the midst of this XL paradigm, it does no good to make ourselves out as the victims and then offer mutual aid and comfort. What's more, as someone born and raised in Asia – which Koolhaas identifies as the source of the XL plague – it is impossible simply to reject or laugh off the XL paradigm as someone else's problem. My intent is to critique Asia, while at the same time accepting its realities, and the realities of myself as someone born there.

I am fascinated by the new physics, which does not adhere to a linear, evolutionary model, moving unidirectionally from small to large, but rather seeks out the small within the large and the large within the small. The new physics is premised on tolerance for multiple layers at different scales, from the subatomic to the cosmically vast, and on the speed required to toggle freely back and forth from the tiny to the enormous.

The world is not evolving unidirectionally toward larger and larger things. Rather, the more that large things grow larger and fast things move faster, the more we are drawn to and enchanted by the small, slow things that are always close at hand (or can be brought closer) and can be grasped directly. In this way, we continually oscillate between the large and the small. The multi-layering of quantum mechanics is not occurring far off in the lofty world of academia, and is a model that aptly describes our everyday experience.

In fact, as buildings get bigger and bigger, the concerns of mindful designers are turning toward smaller and smaller objects. If the goal of architecture in the 20th century was to build large structures efficiently, it is the dialogue and interaction between small things – the points, lines and planes that make up structures – and the human body that have become the central issue in architectural design and technology today. Technologies that employ small, delicate

17 Toyama City Public Library and Glass Art Museum in Toyama prefecture. Japan.

objects to create friendly, liberating spaces have been
emerging one after another.[17]

It is precisely this revival of the XS (extra small) that
I am attempting through the design of small-scale pavilions,
furniture, curtains, products and more.

SUPERSTRING THEORY AND MUSICAL ARCHITECTURE

One could call this concern with smallness a return to
how things were before the Renaissance, before the advent
of size M architecture and the architect as a privileged
authority. Or one could call it a revival of the ethos of the
pre-Raphaelite painters, who sought a return to art before
Raphael (1483–1520), and their successor William Morris,
who spearheaded the Arts and Crafts movement.[18] Arts and
Crafts endeavoured to revert to size S, but got caught in the

18 William Morris Red House. Red House Lane. Bexleyheath. London.

trap of nostalgia, which must be avoided by going beyond
size S, to sizes XS and XXS.

The goal of this book is to take stock of our new quantum-
mechanical environment in which the ultra-small and the
ultra-large are layered, and to explore modes of survival in
this environment. In this, superstring theory was a major
source of insight. Conventional elementary particle theory
considered subatomic particles, envisioned as being like
tiny dots, to be the basic building blocks of the universe.
However, with the discovery of various even more minuscule subatomic particles, such as quarks, photons and
neutrinos, it became difficult to call any kind of particle
the basic unit of the universe.

This challenge was addressed with the formulation of
superstring theory, which holds that all particles actually
take the form of strings. Just as a violin string can produce
a wide variety of sounds when it vibrates, superstring theory
asserts that strings can, for example, sometimes produce
the 'tones' of quarks and sometimes those of neutrinos.

In superstring theory, the cosmos is no longer conceived as an aggregation of matter, but as a vast symphony of various tones and timbres produced by strings. Is it possible to interpret architecture in musical terms as well?

By assuming that everything consists of vibrations, superstring theory overcomes the fundamental obstacle of the point (dot) as a basic model. As a matter of fact, this model was rife with difficulties. If a point comes too close to another point, the force of their gravitational attraction is inversely proportional to the square of the distance between them, and the force acting on them eventually becomes infinite and incalculable. The model of strings and the 'music' they produce surmounts this inherent and inevitable problem. In design, when we simply pursue smallness, from S to XS and so on from there, we are sure to encounter the inevitable problem of the point, but introducing the concepts of vibration and rhythm frees us from this dilemma.

If we define architecture in terms of points or lines, we are immediately confronted with various insoluble issues. This is because neither points nor lines have width or thickness, and no matter how many of them are added together, they will never attain the material mass of a building.

The basic stance of Western architecture was to circumvent these difficulties and define architecture in terms of volumes. In achieving this, the modernist architecture that emerged in 20th-century Europe was the legitimate heir to the European architectural tradition. As a result, architecture lost its innate quantum-mechanical freedom and regressed to the dullness of three-dimensional concrete volumes.

However, once the idea of vibrating strings is introduced, the only difference between a point, a line and a plane is a difference in the quality of vibration, and through vibrations of increasing strength, points, lines and planes can be expanded in any way to form elements of the world. It is possible to extend points, lines and planes into matter, into space and into the cosmos. When we see matter itself as consisting of the vibration, timbre and rhythm of points, lines and planes, architecture and cities take on a completely new appearance.

DELEUZE AND THE RELATIVITY OF MATTER

Introducing the concept of vibration makes it possible to freely traverse points, lines and planes. Even colour, hardness, texture and weight can be explained as the result of vibration. Wassily Kandinsky obviously knew nothing of superstring theory, and was not even familiar with the concept of vibration, but because he was so deeply versed in music, he was intuitively able to connect points, lines and planes as parts of one continuous flow.

Gilles Deleuze's discussion of the relativity of solids and liquids can be seen as an extension of Kandinsky. Using the example of a boat and a wave,[19] Deleuze asserts that water – which we believe to be liquid – sometimes manifests as solid:

'It must be stated that a body has a degree of hardness as well as a degree of fluidity, or that it is essentially elastic, the elastic force of bodies being the expression of the active compressive force exerted on matter. When a boat reaches a certain speed a wave becomes as hard as a wall of marble. The atomistic hypothesis of an absolute hardness and the Cartesian hypothesis of an absolute fluidity are joined all the more because they share the error that posits separable

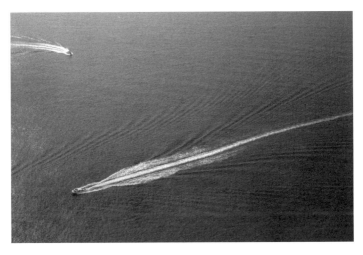

19 Aerial view of boats leaving trails in the sea. Zante. Greece.

minima, either in the form of finite bodies or in infinity in
the form of points.' (Gilles Deleuze, *The Fold: Leibniz and
the Baroque*, 1988.)

Deleuze recognized that matter is fundamentally relativistic or, more appropriately, multi-layered: just as the
expansion of the world around us from size S to XL was
in fact a multi-layering of the world, Deleuze noted that
matter itself is also multi-layered. Deleuze goes on to argue
that matter should be seen not in terms of points, lines,
planes or volumes, but in terms of folds, which are just
vibrations by another name:

'That is what Leibniz explains in an extraordinary
piece of writing… a continuous labyrinth is not a line
dissolving into independent points, as flowing sand might
dissolve into grains, but resembles a sheet of paper divided
into infinite folds or separated into bending movements,
each one determined by the consistent or conspiring
surroundings. "The division of the continuous must not
be taken as of sand dividing into grains, but as that of a

sheet of paper or of a tunic in folds, in such a way that an infinite number of folds can be produced, some smaller than others, but without the body ever dissolving into points or minima"... The unit of matter, the smallest element of the labyrinth, is the fold, not the point which is never a part, but a simple extremity of the line.' (Gilles Deleuze, *The Fold: Leibniz and the Baroque*, 1988.)

Deleuze's conception of matter is another way of saying, as superstring theory does, that the smallest unit of matter is not a point, but the vibration of a string. As one delves into the relativity of matter, one arrives at strings and folds, and matter is redefined as the timbre of their vibrations. As one delves into points, lines and planes, the boundaries between them disappear, and matter is redefined not as an aggregation of points, lines and planes, but as their vibration and resonance.

A remarkable thing about Deleuze's unique discussion of matter is that he drew inspiration for it from Baroque architecture. Deleuze quotes from Heinrich Wölfflin's *Renaissance and Baroque* (1888), a classic of Baroque studies, and ultimately arrives at the conclusion that Baroque buildings are aggregations of innumerable folds.

Just as Kandinsky saw points in Gothic architecture, so Deleuze sees lines in the Baroque, hears the vibrations of the lines and redefines stone structures – which have been thought of as volumes – as aggregations of countless lines. Both Kandinsky and Deleuze were inspired by the leap involved in conceiving heavy, massive and volume-oriented stone as breaking free of material constraints and vibrating to produce the 'music' of points, lines and planes.

How far can we advance beyond this, further into the secrets of vibrating strings and folds? How can we discover, and produce resonance from, contemporary tones that are neither Gothic nor Baroque?

First, I listen closely to the tones emanating from the strings, to the sounds that the materials make. I try plucking the strings and listening to their sounds, and fold them into the depths of my being. Next, I gently touch other strings and make more sounds. And again and again, ad infinitum. We can only repeat this process endlessly, seeking the moment when a new tone rings out. A musician is someone who has the patience to keep up such repetition, and if material is sound, then an architect is also a musician. The most vital thing is to listen, and to continue to listen. In other words, to remain receptive and continue to be patient.

In effect, this book describes the vibrations of strings in three categories: points, lines and planes. Its purpose is not to classify points, lines and planes as such, but on the contrary, to make it clear that points, lines and planes are all vibrations and manifestations thereof, and thus can never truly be divided into separate categories.

POINT

BIG WORLD. LITTLE PEBBLES

When I think of points, or dots, in architecture, the first
thing that comes to mind is stones. Stone is a material that
originally existed as a huge volume, or mass, inside the earth
– so massive and heavy that it could be called equivalent to
the earth itself.[20]

We cut stone into pieces because we cannot handle it as
is. Sometimes we quarry stones and sometimes they are
ground up by the forces of nature and turned into pebbles,
but in both cases they appear to us as points. It is only when
stones are reduced to points that fragile little beings like
us are able to handle them. When we start to think about
stone, we begin to see the relationship between the world
and humankind, and appreciate how big the world is and
how small, weak and unreliable human beings are.

Once stones have been shrunk down to small points,
we stack them up with the structural system known as
masonry. We go through the arduous process of making
them smaller, and then we recombine them once more to
make something larger. Historically, this was the essential
act of architecture (more specifically, masonry is one essential act and wood-frame construction is the other). As far
back as the ancient civilizations of Greece and Rome, the
basis of Western architecture has been masonry, and various
methods of stacking stones, bricks and so forth, one by one,
were the mainstay of European architecture. Meanwhile,
in Asia, wood-frame construction was dominant.

The methods of these two worlds are in contrast, in
the sense that masonry involves piling up points, while

20 Aerial view of Stonehenge. Wiltshire. United Kingdom.

wood-frame construction is based on assembling lines. As a matter of fact, wood-frame construction was originally the basis of ancient Greek architecture, but the Greeks cut down so many trees that their supply of wood ran out, and stonemasonry became the primary approach. This was because unlike the fertile volcanic soil of Japan, the Greek soil was thin and forests could not be regenerated.

However, vestiges of wood-frame construction remain in various details of ancient Greek architecture. The technique of supporting the roof with linear members (rafters), which is characteristic of Asian wood-frame structures, can be seen at ancient Greek sites such as the Parthenon. The memory of rafters – of wood-frame construction and of the forest – were skilfully reproduced by fashioning stone into thin, elongated forms.

Greek temples basically relied on the powerful monumentality of rows of vertical columns, the rhythm of which governed the entire structure. In that sense, ancient Greek architecture was an architecture of columns; of vertical lines. It is clear that the architectural vocabulary of columns originally comes from wood-frame structures.

65

After all, if you cut down a tree in a forest, you have a ready-made column, but it was not easy in ancient times to make columns out of gigantic hunks of stone.

On these grounds, it has repeatedly been asserted that the origins of architecture lay in cutting down trees in the forest and erecting them as columns – Laugier's allegorical engraving, *The Primitive Hut*, appears as the frontispiece in many architectural textbooks to this day. The trees of the forest were clearly revered by human beings, perhaps because we originally arose in forests and depended on them for life.

The basic vocabulary of ancient Greek architecture was organized into five orders (styles of columns). Among them, Doric columns were carved with narrow vertical fluting, reminiscent of bark, and the capitals (tops) of Corinthian columns have acanthus leaves carved into them. Greek architecture did much to reproduce the forest in stone.

FROM GREECE TO ROME

When viewed in this way, ancient Greek architecture, ostensibly based on aggregations of points (stones), was also dependent on lines. The boundary between points and lines is ambiguous, and they are embedded in one another. This delicate ancient Greek architecture, which oscillated back and forth between line and point, was transformed into an architecture of volume by its successor, ancient Rome.

Socially and economically, Rome required massive volumes.[21] The volumetric needs of ancient Rome, which grew into a vast empire spanning multiple continents, dwarfed those of ancient Greece, which consisted of small city-states. The Romans learned much from the Greeks

21 The Maison Carree. a Roman temple in Nimes. France.

and carried on their stylistic legacy, but walls became more important elements than columns – although rows of half-depth columns known as pilasters were attached to massive walls to create rhythm and vibration, they were more or less an ornamental device.

THE SEAGRAM BUILDING AS AN AGGREGATION OF POINTS

During the 20th century, the same thing occurred as in ancient Rome. Modernist architecture, which started from a 'small place' (Europe), initially emphasized lines as the Greek temples had. The rhythms created by these lines, in the forms of columns, were used as an organizing principle for the entirety of structures.

However, as the economic centre of the world shifted from Europe to the United States after World War I, the

67

22 Mies van der Rohes Barcelona Pavilion. Catalonia. Spain.

expansion of volumes became the goal of society and the theme of architectural design. While Europe was a 'small place' like ancient Greece, the US was a 'big place' like the Roman Empire and ancient history repeated itself.

As with the columns of Rome, Mies van der Rohe attempted to imbue gargantuan structures with a sense of rhythm by applying columns to massive volumes.[22] Mies himself moved from Europe to the US in 1938, an event symbolizing the shift of architecture's centre from Europe to the US. Mies correctly understood the essence and significance of this move, and adapted his designs to the 'big place' that was his new home.

Mies's Seagram Building was considered a masterwork of the skyscraper form, but architectural historian Reyner Banham notes that the Seagram Building became a modernist masterpiece due to its successful updating of the masonry paradigm. In masonry each of the stones – the units forming the mass – are clearly recognizable, and those units (points) cannot exceed the size of what the human body can handle. In other words, the body defines the size of the points that are the units of masonry. People find masonry structures familiar and friendly due to the intimate scale of the points.

Similarly, a bronze framework divides the glass curtain wall of the Seagram Building into small points. Mies also fixed bronze frames to stone walls lacking glass, and as Banham notes, these were not columns added merely for decorative purposes, rather the entire building was designed to be an aggregation of minuscule points. Mies was the son of a stone carver, and according to Banham this was reflected in his transforming a skyscraper into a collection of human-scale points with a masonry-derived approach. It was Banham's insights into the Seagram Building that initially sparked my exploration of points.

Devices like that of Mies can be found in many ancient structures as well. In the case of masonry, the units (points) must be packed close together with no spaces between them to support the building, and the resulting whole emerges as a heavy, massive volume. While the basic unit is the point, the point's lightness vanishes from the finished product. To avoid this pitfall, both the Greeks and the Romans made V-shaped cuts in the joints between stones to generate large shadows, or gave the surfaces of stones a rough finish to make each stone feel like an independent point.

THE CHALLENGE OF POINTS IN
THE DESIGN OF STONE PLAZA

Stone is a tricky material that, while essentially consisting of points, is easily connected to become a monolithic volume. Stone Plaza (2000) was created in collaboration with Shirai Sekizai Co., which has its own quarry for Ashino stone. It was the first project on which I grappled with this challenging material, and as Stone Plaza[23] is a museum dedicated to stone, I was strongly encouraged to use stone from the local area in the design. I had always steered clear of stone, because it is a perilous material that can easily lead one into the pitfalls of volume.

I absolutely wanted to avoid the most common method today, which is to apply a thin layer of stone over concrete. Applying a thin, textured finishing material on top of concrete, and then touching up or refinishing the surface material as necessary, prevailed during the 20th century as a means of concealing the appearance of blocky, mono-lithic volumes. As a thin surface layer of stone would make a building look luxurious and cause condominiums to sell for higher prices, stone cut into thin slices was consumed in vast quantities.

However, I wanted to somehow rescue stone's richness as a material from this impoverished state dominated by cosmetic and semiotic concerns. After all, the history of stone is as long as that of the planet itself. We arrived at two methods for Stone Plaza. One was to treat pieces of stone as louvres (lines). With these linear elements, we sought to save the stone from becoming a bulky volume. This required

23 Stone Plaza 2000 . Nasu. Japan. At the centre of the water pool. a 100-year-old storehouse for rice is juxtaposed with a group of galleries. stacked up with newly designed details.

linear steel supports to hold the louvres in place, resulting in a configuration like the warp and weft of textiles, with horizontals and verticals woven together.

The other new method we employed at Stone Plaza was to lay the stones like bricks, thereby preventing them from fusing into a volume. To this end, we laid the stones with gaps between them. Here, the challenge was to somehow turn stones back into point-units by increasing the number of gaps, but when masonry becomes so highly porous, is it still masonry? While repeatedly asking myself this question, I drew gradually closer to the goal of working with points.

However, even with all these gaps, the stone still needed to have seismic resistance. Katsuo Nakata, a structural engineer, advised me that even if one-third of the stones were removed, a stone structural wall could still withstand an earthquake, although this one-third figure was based on intuition, not calculation. While this seemed like an unscientific comment coming from an engineer, I began a study on the removal of stones, using one-third as a benchmark.

Carefully reviewing the section on masonry in the Japanese Building Standards Act, I was surprised to find that the masonry regulations themselves are vague. There are standards for the lengths and thicknesses of walls, but no clear grounds are given for these standards, only vague, experientially based ones: in effect, 'this standard has been applied and structures have not collapsed so far, so it must be all right'.

THE JUMP FROM POINT TO VOLUME

This vagueness is not limited to the Japanese Building Standards Act. The seismic resistance of masonry construction in general is not confirmed through calculations, but depends on experience. This is because it entails piling up many small points to form a large volume, which is a process shrouded in mystery and still reliant on experience. It requires a magical jump: even in the 21st century, people still rely on 'magic' in their handling of points.

By contrast, structures composed of frames, such as columns and beams, are based on formulas. Lines are computable, and that is why architecture based on frames (lines) became prevalent in the 20th century.[24] With frames, it is possible to make calculations even with quite primitive methods.

As construction became more sophisticated, so too did the calculations and the calculation methods used. Prior to the 19th century, the concept of structural calculation did not exist. Everything depended on experience, as Europe was dominated by masonry – the aggregations of points that were impossible to calculate in the first place. However, in the 20th century, linear elements such as steel frames and

24 Masonry detail for Stone Plaza.

concrete columns were introduced into European architecture, and the work of structural calculation began.

Initially, only frame analysis was possible, in which calculations were carried out as if buildings were simple frames. Only a simple type of frame known as a rigid frame could be subjected to calculation, so architects designed large numbers of rigid-frame buildings, obediently staying within the limits prescribed by computation. In this way, the computational limits imposed restrictions on reality.

It was only fairly recently that we finally became able to increase the numbers of points and lines, and calculate more complex frames using the finite element method. Thanks to computers, calculations have evolved further, from the finite element method, to the discrete element method, to the particle method, and it is finally possible to handle particles (small points). While lines were easy to handle, points had long been mysterious entities, but computational technology now underpins our architectural designs, which resemble aggregations of particles.

Returning to Stone Plaza, the simple act of pulling out one-third of the stones made the stone wall – which one would expect to be a volume – appear as an aggregation of disparate points. This was a mysterious and quite magical experience.

There are two ways to deal with the removal of parts. One is to leave holes where the stones were removed. Naturally, this lets in light and air currents, making it impossible to air-condition the interior, which would render this approach unfeasible for an ordinary museum. However, as the exhibits here were to consist of stone sculptures and crafts, it was decided that air conditioning would not be used. This was a detail that critiqued the 20th-century, US-style architectural model of a completely enclosed, fully air-conditioned volume.

Another challenging detail was fitting thinly sliced stone into holes from which stones had been extracted. Bianco Carrara is a variety of Italian marble that came into use after the Roman Emperor, Julius Caesar, opened a quarry on the mountains of Carrara. In ancient Rome, glass was so expensive that in Roman baths, such as the Baths of Caracalla, thinly sliced stone was fitted into the openings instead. Roman windows, too, were made of stone rather than glass.

Carrara stone remains the most widely used stone in the world today, and when sliced to a thickness of 6 mm (¼ in.) it allows light to pass through. Fitting this thinly sliced stone where panes of glass might ordinarily go enabled the entire Stone Plaza structure to become an aggregation of stones as small points. The principle of points was thoroughly implemented and the interior was bathed in wonderful light filtered through Bianco Carrara.

The plane could be called a product of the modern era, as historically, producing a plane required a high level of skill.

In pre-modern times, glass – which we think of as a planar material – could only be produced at sizes so small they could be more aptly described as points. In medieval European buildings, windows were divided into small sections with lead frames and fitted with small panes of glass.

In the middle of each small glass pane is a circular protrusion like a lens. This is because it was not possible to make large planes of glass at the time. Instead, glass was blown to make vessels that were then split and flattened to produce glass plates, creating these strange protuberances in the process. The points (units), made by blowing glass and then splitting it, were joined together with lead. Even if apertures themselves grew larger, each aperture remained an aggregation of points and stayed at a human scale. It was not until much later that it became possible to make large panes of glass.

For a very long time, walls and apertures were issues that people could only resolve using points, and we strug-gled to somehow connect to the world at large through the medium of these small points. It is often moving to see the vestiges of these struggles, such as the protrusions on medieval glass windows.

Stone Plaza was a turning point for me in many ways. First of all, it was there that I first encountered stone, and gained the opportunity to engage with the profound world of this material. This encounter with stone, which has a tendency to become a hefty volume, made me aware of the significance and value of points, and led me to start focusing on them. For me, stone opened the door to the world of points.

THE BLUE STONE OF BRUNELLESCHI

Stone Plaza was built with Ashino stone that was created by a volcanic eruption four billion years ago, and it was this material that led me to the world of points. After that, I encountered Pietra Serena, a blue-tinted grey sandstone from quarries on the outskirts of Florence, which further deepened that world.

Salvatore, a stonemason who owns a Pietra Serena quarry, came all the way from Italy to visit our office, asking us to design a small pavilion using Pietra Serena. The stone, which he had packed in a suitcase and brought with him, was a tranquil shade of blue-grey well suited to its name, which means 'pure stone'. I liked it at first sight.

Steve Jobs had a special fondness for Pietra Serena, and gave strict orders that the floors of every Apple Store in every city were to be finished in this stone. Looking further back in history we can see that this stone's role in architecture is surprisingly large and deep.

Filippo Brunelleschi (1377–1446) is considered the first architect of the Renaissance. He was based in Florence near a Pietra Serena quarry and prized the stone for his work, using it in a unique and unprecedented way. First, he designed the structural frame (columns, beams and arches) to be made with Pietra Serena, and then he filled the gaps between the frame elements with plain white plastered walls.[25] His actual buildings were designed to resemble frames line-drawn with a pen on a white sheet of paper.

However, Brunelleschi's buildings were not actually supported by these frames, but by the structural system

25 Ospedale degli Innocenti　Hospital of the Innocents. Piazza della Santissima Annunziata. Florence. Italy.

– masonry walls – that were common at the time. It was not until the 19th century that structural frames made of concrete and steel began to support buildings. A frame structure was, in other words, a linear framework rather than a volume. Until the 19th century, masonry was the predominant method of building in Europe, and in the 15th century Brunelleschi had no choice but to construct buildings with the heavy, closed volumes unique to masonry, due to the technical constraints of the approach.

Within these constraints, however, Brunelleschi dreamed of an architecture of lines. He used Pietra Serena to produce frameworks of thin lines on the white plaster walls, with the stone's distinctive bluish-grey tones well suited to rendering sharp lines. He tried to give his build-ings a mathematical and abstract atmosphere, as if he had etched the lines in blue ink on white paper. Long before steel structures were built, he used the pale tones of Pietra Serena to present an architecture of lines.

Michelangelo (1475–1564) was born almost 100 years after Brunelleschi and was a central figure in the Renaissance at its zenith. He was similarly fond of Pietra Serena. In the hall of the Laurentian Library (Biblioteca Medicea Laurenziana or BML) a blue Pietra Serena staircase seems to float within a frame, also of Pietra Serena, against a white wall. This has been said to be the world's most beautiful staircase.

Although they were constrained by the masonry techniques of their time, both Brunelleschi and Michelangelo created architectures of line that foretold the coming age of the structural frame – the age of the line. They were prophets of the line, and the cool blue-grey surface of Pietra Serena – quarried from mountains near Florence, where they were active – was chosen as the ideal substance to manifest this prophecy. The architects' mathematical, abstract ideas were linked to familiar local materials, demonstrating how architecture connects local sites to the entire cosmos, and the material to the conceptual.

The age of the frame arrived 300 years later, and by the late 19th century steel and concrete frames supported buildings, with the spaces within the frames filled with glass or wall material. The technology of the line made skyscrapers possible, and gave rise to the cities and civilizations of the 20th century. The prophecy that Brunelleschi and Michelangelo presented using the medium of Pietra Serena had a range of several centuries.

BRUNELLESCHI'S INNOVATIONS
WITH POINTS

Brunelleschi was not only a pioneer in the transition from volume (masonry) to line, but also experimented with points in intriguing ways. The large cupola (dome) above the Florentine cathedral Basilica di Santa Maria del Fiore, considered to be his masterpiece and famous for the technological breakthroughs it achieved in the design of domes, was a large-scale innovation that explored the possibilities of the point.

Countless domes have been built throughout history, as a means of simultaneously creating large, dynamic interior spaces free of columns and symbolic exteriors that reach for the heavens. The dome has been used since ancient times as a means of obtaining large volumes, by stacking up small points of stone and brick.

However, the weight of stones and bricks placed limitations on a dome's size. Both stone and brick have weak adhesive surfaces between points (individual units) compared to the weight of the material, and tend to collapse under their own weight. The fact that each of the points possessed such weight constituted a fatal flaw, and in medieval times it was considered impossible to create a dome with a diameter of more than 30 metres (98 feet). In other words, there was a physical limit to the jump from point to volume – the sublimation of one to the other – and the maximum diameter of 30 metres (98 feet) could not be exceeded, no matter how much ingenuity went into stone and brick masonry.

This constraint was overcome with the great cupola of Santa Maria del Fiore and the genius of Brunelleschi. The proud Florentines felt that the cathedral's compact, medieval dome was inadequate for Florence, which had become Italy's economic and cultural hub thanks to its textile and financial industries.

In 1418, the Florentine government held a competition for a new dome design, and Brunelleschi submitted a bold proposal that was so groundbreaking and controversial that he won the competition. He did not live to see the dome completed in person, but based on his proposal an enormous volume suitable to represent the 'city of flowers' was created, measuring 43 metres (141 feet) in diameter and 120 metres (394 feet) in height. The fact that it was realized posthumously indicates the difficult and visionary nature of the proposal.

What made the large dome possible was the idea of a double dome with a framework of ribs.[26] Through the intervention of ribs (lines), point and volume are smoothly connected, not directly but hierarchically. Brunelleschi was the first architect to realize the potential of the line, and his concern and obsession with line can be seen in all of his works, including the Hospital of the Innocents with its facade of lines rendered in Pietra Serena stone.

However, while Brunelleschi intuitively understood that line could be a medium that smoothly connected point and volume, he obtained specific clues to back up this intuition through an encounter with ancient Rome. After the cupola competition was officially proclaimed, Brunelleschi visited Roman ruins to study the Roman orders, as exemplified by Doric, Ionic and Corinthian columns. He discovered that ancient Roman architecture employed lines in the form of columns, both structurally and in terms of design, to realize

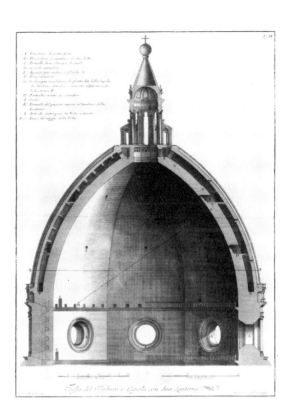

26 The interior design for the dome of Florence Cathedral. Italy.

enormous volumes. Ancient Roman architecture developed the idea of the line, which had originated in Greece, to the maximum extent so as to obtain the colossal volumes demanded by the society of Rome as it burgeoned into a world-spanning empire.

Linear elements of pilasters (colonnades) were added to huge, often blank and expressionless wall surfaces, and the Romans devised gigantic columns that spanned two or more stories, in what was called the 'giant order', in order to unify architectural forms. The long lines of the giant order made it possible to give large, tall buildings rhythmic designs without excess elongation, solving the issue of the huge volumes required by the expanding Roman society.

Having discovered the lines in the Roman ruins, Brunelleschi applied them to the Florentine dome competition. In Santa Maria del Fiore, lines were combined and woven together in various ways to strengthen the building's structure. First, a ring was made by joining 60 wooden timbers (clearly an example of line) with iron strips (again, line) and bolts. The ring – itself a line – cinched the bottom of the dome and kept it from collapsing horizontally.

The ribbed dome was double-layered for further reinforcement, and by weaving together two layers of ribs (lines) the dome was freed from its 30-metre (98-foot) limit. In this way, the weaknesses of points were overcome through lines, and the lines gained additional strength by being interwoven. This architectural innovation was perfectly befitting for Florence, a city that had flourished through the textile industry – the art of weaving lines – and is where we see the emergence of the prioritization of volume above all else, which led to the skyscrapers of the 20th century.

BRUNELLESCHI'S INDUCTIVE ARCHITECTURE

Another novel aspect of Filippo Brunelleschi's competition proposal was its innovative construction approach, which called for building the dome without scaffolding. Even if lines (in the form of ribs) were introduced as an intermediary between point and volume, spaces between the ribs still needed to be slowly and gradually filled with points (bricks). This meant that a great leap was required to forcefully connect point and volume.

Cast-in-place concrete, which became the most common construction method of the 20th century, was a fantastic

means of jumping from tiny points (gravel, sand, cement)
to volumes all at once, while eliminating the need to lay
individual stones or bricks by hand. In this sense, concrete
was both a magical and a lazy construction method, and
people in the 20th century were so enthusiastic about it
that they abandoned themselves to it like drug addicts.

The jump from point to line in concrete was possible only
through the use of temporary scaffolding – an auxiliary
structure resembling the stagehands in a play.[27] Without
scaffolding, concrete construction would never have been
possible, and it was precisely because temporary scaffolding could be produced so easily that cast-in-place concrete
dominated the 20th century. Scaffolding, which consists
of lines, enabled points to make the jump to volumes.

However, to build a dome in the 15th century meant constructing a temporary wooden scaffolding that was the same size as the dome itself. This scaffolding had to be erected under the dome, with dome-shaped wooden formwork built on top of it, upon which bricks could be then laid. This was far more labour-intensive than putting up scaffolding to build a vertical wall, and the entire interior of the dome would be filled with a forest of temporary scaffolding.

Brunelleschi intrepidly challenged the status quo by devising a process in which scaffolding could be omitted entirely. To achieve this, Brunelleschi redesigned the bricks themselves so that they were thin, but with a large horizontal surface area. He also shifted the positions of the bricks so they could be cantilevered, which made it possible to stagger the bricks significantly from one level to the next. These broad, flattened bricks – sometimes called '*konnyaku* bricks' in Japan, because of their resemblance to the slabs in which that eponymous jellied root vegetable is sold – are still points, but have also come slightly closer to being lines.

In addition, Brunelleschi introduced a zigzag bricklaying technique known as herringbone, which boosts the strength of the bonds between bricks. Herringbone is another sophisticated technique that subtly introduces lines into the realm of points. It ingeniously made aggregations of points even stronger and more tenacious than before, just as the literal bones of a herring hold the fish's flesh together. The herringbone was the result of studying which structures of bones (lines) could be inserted to form the strongest and most flexible body.

This staggered bricklaying was carried out in curves along the horizontal circumference of the dome, and through this rotation a small degree of staggering created a large degree of shift and cantilevering as successive circles of bricks were laid. This made it possible to construct a large dome in a safe and economical manner without using any scaffolding whatsoever.

This was a breakthrough that resembles induction in mathematics. The logic of inductive reasoning is that if you can show that what is true for n is also true for $n+1$, then all you have to do is repeat this procedure indefinitely. By applying induction to architecture, Brunelleschi eliminated the need for troublesome scaffolding.

DEDUCTIVE AND INDUCTIVE ARCHITECTURE

In architecture there are both deductive and inductive approaches. The concrete architecture of the 20th century is deductive: it starts with an image of the overall form and the materials that make up the components and details of the whole are then selected to realize that form. The parts are subordinate to the whole.

Brunelleschi's method, by contrast, is inductive, in that it endeavours to start with the parts and arrive at the whole. After thoroughly investigating the properties and limitations of the parts, these parts are interconnected and the process advances to the next level. Sometimes, an unexpected whole emerges from the iteration of work procedures, which is evidence that the process is inductive. Inductive methods will be used more frequently in the architecture of the future because induction is compatible with the additive architecture enabled by computational design.

28 Staircases and atrium interior of the Bradbury Building. Downtown Los Angeles. USA.

Brunelleschi understood the effects of induction; he
extended the point inductively to arrive at the line. He also
thoroughly understood the effects of lines, and utilized
them to the fullest extent. To me, this seems related to the
fact that he started his career as a goldsmith, and was originally educated in the techniques of goldsmithing rather
than those of architecture. Whereas stones and bricks are
essentially points, metal essentially consists of lines and
planes. His experiences with gold taught him the magic of
the line, and he took this magic with him when he entered
the field of architecture.

The history of architecture from Brunelleschi onward
was opened up by the introduction of a new material: metal.
The effects of metal on the history of architecture were
transformational, because metal and the line are insep-
arable. The lines that iron and steel produce – including
cast-iron columns[28] – enabled the creation of large spaces,
expanding the scale of architecture. To paraphrase the

German Chancellor Otto von Bismarck (1815–1898), 'the great questions of the day will be settled by iron and blood' – testament to the crucial role of linear metal in the expansion of built environments. Indeed, iron played a major role in Germany flourishing in the 19th century.

Concrete, which appears unrelated to metal, could not be used to build structures without the reinforcing steel bars (rebar) concealed inside it. Minuscule points of sand, gravel, cement and so forth are bound into a solid whole by lines of rebar. Therefore, the modernization of architecture was synonymous with its adoption of the metallic and the linear, and the first step was Brunelleschi's transition from goldsmithing to architecture.

PLASTIC CONTAINERS AND CADDISFLIES

It was from Brunelleschi that I learned how staggering could inductively transform points into lines, and I first attempted to build a masonry structure by stacking points in a pavilion I called Water Block House (2006). Two years later, in another pavilion, Water Branch House (2008), I introduced staggering in a Brunelleschi-style evolution, endeavouring to vicariously experience his journey from point to line.

The pavilion was inspired by a barricade made of stacked plastic containers. When the lightweight empty plastic containers are brought in and filled with water on site, they are transformed into units of a heavy barricade and will not topple over, even in strong wind. To move the structure to a new location, all you have to do is drain the water out again.

This struck me as a certain kind of architectural wizardry, in which the weight of the points could be changed freely.

Everyone believes buildings, once built, are immovable and unchanging in shape; completed buildings are supposed to remain the same in terms of form, weight and all other aspects. However, the barricades of plastic containers used at construction sites seemed to be a bold challenge to this conventional wisdom, which I found thrilling. How could these small points of variable weight be assembled to create new types of structures?

The first idea that came to mind was that of Water Branch House,[29] which was constructed using the 'Lego brick' method. Lego bricks were, fittingly, invented in Europe (specifically Denmark), the home of masonry, and employ the point-based method of bricklaying and stonemasonry. But, instead of the conventional method of joining bricks with adhesives such as mortar, the interlocking pieces are connected with studs and indentations – a mechanism used in wood joinery. A similar convex-concave joint is also used for the lids of small wood seal cases, which many Japanese TV viewers will know from the period drama *Mito Komon*. This is known as *inrotsugi* ('seal case joinery') in Japan.

The Lego Group's precursor was a Danish carpentry business, and Lego is a synthesis of woodworking concepts inherited from that business and the stacking system of masonry. Yet while it is easy to build vertical walls using Lego, it is more difficult to put on a roof, and if a roof could not be added to Water Branch House, it would be impossible to build it using only plastic containers. Instead, the walls would need to be bridged with wooden beams, and this outcome would be the same as a Western brick or stone building, in which wood framing is used for the floor and roof. Our goal was to create a mathematical pavilion that could be assembled entirely from a single type of unit: if a pavilion cannot be built without relying on different

29 Water Branch House 2008 . We assembled small units and covered them with a tarpaulin as if putting a raincoat.

components, it will not be versatile and will not be a beautiful, mathematical feat of engineering.

The beauty of an animal's nest is that it is an entire structure built of only one type of unit and completed with a single repeated action. A fascinating example of this is the nest of the caddisfly, small insect aquatic larvae of the order Trichoptera. Caddisflies rely on only one action, the rotation of their bodies, to create their nests. The materials available are different in each location, so the nests take on different appearances, but each uses only one action and one method. They are nests, but at the same time they are like garments for the larvae, or parts of their own bodies.

The simplicity of the method and lack of hesitation make the architecture of the caddisflies' nests seem as natural as their bodies. For a long time I admired caddisflies, and wanted to emulate them by designing body-like structures; their versatility and openness to using whatever small 'points' are close at hand is also appealing. In the 20th century, using the cheapest materials, often transported from far away, became the basic rule of architecture, and the large quantities of CO_2 emitted during transport were not considered a problem. As a result, architecture became homogenized and lost its sense of regionalism. We must regain our sense of place by taking a cue from caddisflies and returning to readily available materials (points).

Inspired by both caddisflies and Brunelleschi, I devised Water Branches: elongated plastic containers with a blocky zigzag form. The idea for the branch-like shape came when I was asked by the Museum of Modern Art, New York (MoMA) to participate in their exhibition 'Home Delivery: Fabricating the Modern Dwelling', which focuses on structures that can be built with the ease of ordering a pizza delivery. I thought that this called for a form and a method like those of caddisfly nests. The container reminded me of a tree branch, so instead of a block I named it a Water Branch.

Like the large, flattened bricks designed by Brunelleschi, the Water Branch is a little closer to being a 'line', which meant the branches could be stacked in a staggered formation. Branches could be shifted freely in either direction, resulting in something that was not so much staggering, but more a vertical and horizontal weaving of linear forms. While seeking to connect the point to the world around us, I somehow arrived at a line, and was beginning to weave these lines together. By jumping from point to line, and working with lines as the basic units, it became easier to bring a structure into the world.

I found it interesting that Water Branches were somewhere between points and lines. They were a little too short and incomplete to be lines, so in this sense they are 'line segments'. This has its advantages, as long, linear objects are difficult to transport and assemble, whereas line segments make both transportation and construction far easier.

CONNECTING POINTS WITH LIQUID

With the Water Branch, I started seeking ways to connect point to line, and there was another major leap achieved with Water Branch House: the connection of branch to branch, or point to point, with liquid (water).

As the name suggests, a Water Block unit can be filled with water, but the water is enclosed and capped so it cannot flow from one unit to another. In Water Branch House, however, the branches are interlocking, and water flows freely through them; water flows through the walls, floor and roof of the structure, and the branches are thoroughly interconnected by water.[30]

There is a major difference between flowing and non-flowing water, which is as huge as the difference between life and death. With Water Branch House, heat collectors were constructed out of branches and placed outside the pavilion. Sunlight warmed the water, which was then circulated through Water Branch House. Just as blood circulates around the human body and warms it, the floor, walls and roof built of Water Branches gradually grew warmer. With flowing water, a vital phenomenon that occurs in the body was realized in the hard, static world of architecture.

As liquid flowed through it, Water Branch House seemed to transcend individual lines and become a single piece of fabric (a single plane). The liquid created a relationship in which point, line and plane were reciprocally embedded, and one could say that the units (points) in Water Branch House were linked by liquid and by flow.

30 Detail of Water Branch House. Connecting the small units with vinyl pipes enables the liquid to flow inside the units.

Buildings usually belong to the world of solids, but in the biological realm, the points known as cells are often connected to other cells by the flow of liquid. An organism is both a solid and a liquid, and it is through liquid that it stays strong and structurally integrated, while energy and information are exchanged through the fluid medium. The mark of a living thing is that it is connected, point to point, cell to cell, simply by the presence of liquid, without necessarily needing the intervention of pipes such as blood vessels.

Through this project I gained a renewed understanding of how liquid plays a crucial role in linking points in the world of organic life. It is time for the world of architecture, too, to graduate from the world of solids and enter the world of liquids. In built environments, liquid still flows only through pipes, but if liquid itself becomes the main actor, then maybe architecture can make the leap to a new dimension.

METABOLISM AND POINTS

In the architectural field, the Metabolism movement that emerged in Japan in the 1960s exemplified the pursuit of biological phenomena and living organisms as models. The movement's name references the metabolism of living organisms, and the Metabolist architects – Takashi Asada, Kiyonori Kikutake, Kisho Kurokawa, Masato Otaka, Kenji Ekuan, Kiyoshi Awazu and Fumihiko Maki – asserted that built environments must also be able to metabolize smoothly in response to changes in society, usage and scale. In place of the disposable, scrap-and-build paradigm, they set forth a vision in which buildings would slowly evolve as modular units were replaced, added or subtracted.

The Metabolist Manifesto was published in 1959, just as Japan was entering its peak period of rapid economic growth. The bold proposals and designs of these young architects, which seemed to anticipate the era of environmental awareness, drew high acclaim overseas, and the international profiles of Japanese architects rose swiftly. However, while the drawings were excellent, the Metabolist projects that were actually realized disappointed many, and the movement was short-lived.

I believe one major reason for this was the use of the capsule, a large 'point', as a structural unit. They aimed to make buildings metabolize by constructing offices, residences and hotels with capsules as units, and replacing these capsules as needed. However, this metabolism – the replacement of capsules – was extremely challenging in practical, physical terms. It was difficult to transport large

31 Nakagin Capsule Tower. Tokyo. Japan.

cranes to urban sites to remove and install heavy capsules, and reconnecting the main piping network to the piping that connected the capsules was also a stumbling block. It is telling that Kisho Kurokawa's Nakagin Capsule Tower (1972),[31] a flagship work of Metabolism, has not had a single capsule replaced since its completion, and metabolism through capsules came to be derided as nothing more than an architect's delusion.

Metabolism failed because its metabolic units were too large, as the biologist Shin-ichi Fukuoka has also pointed out. The idea of replacing capsules is as far-fetched as the idea that we could easily replace organs in living bodies.

Organ transplantation does occur, but it is a harsh procedure devised as a last resort by modern medicine, and transferring organs from one living thing to another does not occur in nature.

Fukuoka notes that living organisms slowly and continuously metabolize through the gradual replacement of the microscopic points we call cells. As Fukuoka says, life is flow, and contemporary biology has arrived at the view that all things achieve dynamic equilibrium in the context of this flow. Until the early 20th century, biology viewed organisms as being in static equilibrium, with their basic units being the large 'points' of their organs. This view is now thoroughly obsolete.

The 'body without organs' conceived by the poet Antonin Artaud (1896–1948) was adopted as one of the central concepts of Deleuze and Guattari's *Anti-Oedipus* (1972), in which they critiqued the organ-based biological paradigm. As units, organs are too large, as are capsules. However, if we can make points smaller and smaller, and utilize the liquids and gases around solid points as mediums, then architectural Metabolism, which once failed, may rise again.

The liquid-connected Water Branch House is conceived as a first step towards this new Metabolism, in which buildings must not be static, but must continue to flow. Bricks and concrete blocks are also small, discrete points, but replacing individual points requires a major, violent operation that entails the removal of the mortar that holds them together. There must also be air-conditioning ducts and pipes for plumbing and hot water, which may also need to be removed, relocated or replaced.

Water Branch House, by contrast, uses liquid as a medium to exchange heat and energy, so no ducts or pipes are needed. Kurosawa's capsule-based Nakagin apartment building always faced the obstacle of replacing ducts and pipes should a capsule be added or removed, but if small points (units) are connected through a liquid medium, they can be joined without adhesives such as mortar, and without any ducts or pipes; they can constitute a single body. Metabolism attempted to learn from biology, but the learning process was simplistic. However, looking beyond Water Branch House, the creation of a new biological architecture is certainly within our reach.

STONE SLICED THINNER THAN WOOD

Let us return to Brunelleschi's beloved Pietra Serena stone. Salvatore, a stonemason and owner of a quarry from which this stone is sourced, asked me to design a pavilion using the material. I looked for a way to make the stone, which had been treated as points, leap directly to linearity, but Brunelleschi's technique of staggered masonry wasn't an option, as it would inevitably make the pavilion too heavy; Salvatore was looking for a light pavilion that could be transported. However, if we could create lines with the stone by slicing it as thinly as possible, and then assemble those lines into a structure, we might just be able to fulfil the stonemason's challenging request.

A stroke of inspiration came from the classic 'house of cards', in which triangles of playing cards are stacked to form a pyramid. Even the thinnest and most unreliable lines can produce a solid structure if the structural stability of triangles is applied.

Truss structures,[32] in which linear materials such as steel and wooden beams are assembled to create a stable structure, have been in use since ancient Roman times, and

32 Roof truss on a residential construction site in Oregon. USA.

splendidly utilize the principle of the triangle. Since both wood and steel are limited in length, they are not exactly lines, but line segments that lie somewhere between points and lines.

The same method was employed with the Pietra Serena 'house of cards'. The Italian stonemasons cut the stone with a dexterity matching that of Japanese carpenters, slicing it so thinly that it could be called a line, which enabled the truss principle to be applied. The result was a transparent house-of-cards pavilion that was sturdy despite being made with thin stone.

JAPANESE AND CHINESE ROOF TILES

Encounters with new materials lead us to new stages of development, as was the case when I rediscovered Brunelleschi's conflict between point and line after encountering Pietra Serena. New materials always appear to us as unfamiliar, but by engaging and working with them we can advance into new territory. In that sense, the roof tiles of Chinese houses were unfamiliar to me, so my encounter with them marked the beginning of a new phase in the architecture of points.

Designing buildings in China is not easy, and demanding the same level of precision as in Japan is a recipe for disaster. The materials that arrive at the building site vary so widely that most Japanese architects are at a loss when faced with such inconsistency, and that's before they even consider the precision of construction. When I first started working in China I was repeatedly discouraged and devastated by what I encountered.

One day, however, my attitude changed. I made a 180-degree turn, thinking there must be a way to design things so that inconsistency became a benefit, rather than a disadvantage. Once I started thinking along these lines, I came to enjoy working in China precisely because there were inconsistencies everywhere I looked. Eventually, I began seeking out even more extreme inconsistencies, and among my favourite things that I found were the roof tiles used for Chinese houses, which are extraordinarily varied, with a fascinating variety of colours, shapes and sizes.[33]

33 Decorative carved wooden detail and *hongawara* roof tiles on exterior of Ninomaru Palace. Kyoto. Japan.

I thoroughly explored the potential of these tiles in two museums: one in Hangzhou and the other in Xinjin. In both places, the building sites were surrounded by classic Chinese pastoral scenery, and traditional houses with tiled roofs were the basic units of the landscape. In this rural environment, columns of white smoke could sometimes be seen rising from kilns where roof tiles are fired. Even today, small, primitive, earth-and-brick kilns are constructed in fields and the roof tiles are fired by burning wood, which explains why the tiles are so richly varied.

By contrast, most Japanese roof tiles are fired by machine in large factories, so naturally there is little variation; inconsistency is unacceptable. Japanese meticulousness and advanced industrial technology have come together to achieve a level of precision and uniformity that stands in stark contrast to the anything-goes quality of Chinese roof tiles.

As a result, the roofs of Japanese houses have become quite bland. Tiles are living points, and the rhythm generated by

99

these points should make a roof expressive and give a sense of scale, but Japanese tiles – which are now industrial products – convey no sense of constituting 'points'. Japanese tiled roofs look like any old roof painted grey, and the rhythm and dynamism of points are nowhere to be found.

The shapes of the roof tiles add to this sense of flatness. Originally, tiled roofs were made with ceramic tiles that were shaped into curved planar forms before firing, and laid in a pattern of alternating upward- and downward-facing tiles to repel rainwater. European and Asian roof tiles both started with this basic form and, in Japan, the upward-facing tiles, known as *hongawara*, were made to have a dramatically arched convex curve so the shadows cast by concave and convex planes were more clearly defined.

Since the Nara Period (710–794), the *hongawara* tile has been one of the basic elements of the Japanese urban landscape. However, in 1674, during the Edo Period (1603–1868), Nishimura Gohei Masateru, a tile artisan in Omi Province, invented a streamlined economical system in which a single tile, known as *sangawara*, combined the broad, flat concave *hiragawara* and the semi-cylindrical convex *marugawara*.

Although this new tile improved the efficiency of construction, it also meant that Japanese roofs lost all their shadows and drama, and have become bland and featureless. The *sangawara* tile became even more uniform due to industrialization and homogenization after the Meiji Restoration (1868), and Japanese roofs have become duller still. The sparkle and rhythm of points have completely disappeared from Japanese roofs, and from Japan's scenery as a whole.

Fed up with this blandness, I found the variety emanating from the points of Chinese roof tiles to be miraculously beautiful and vibrant. I harboured a secret hope that if I were to design something in the Chinese countryside, I would make these tiles, hand-fired in fields, the project's most prominent feature.

POINT DISTRIBUTION AND AGEING

The site of the China Academy of Art's Folk Art Museum in Hangzhou was originally a tea plantation, and the idea was to construct a building that would nestle against the gently sloping ground that is characteristic of tea plantations, and roof it entirely with tiles. However, simply roofing the building with tiles would not automatically make it blend in with the landscape. If a roof is too large, the size of each tile (or point) that makes up the roof will be too small compared to the overall surface area, and no matter how random the variations among those points may be, the points will be buried within the larger surface, creating an impression of flatness.

To avoid this pitfall, I felt the project should have the look of a village, with numerous small roofs on a scale resembling that of a private house,[34] rather than building fewer, larger roofs. When arrayed on these small roofs, the multifarious tiles would assert themselves as fully independent points, without being swallowed up by the whole.

When designing architecture of points, the crucial matter is the balance between the points and the whole. To achieve this balance, I often create hierarchies of points, connecting them step by step to the whole, and then to the surrounding environment. In this case, small rhomboid planar spaces that fit under each small roof trace the subtly sloping topography of the former tea fields using the polygon

34 China Academy of Art's Folk Art Museum (2015). Hangzhou, China. The museum was built along a hill that used to be a tea plantation.

division method, which approximates a complex curved surface as a collection of triangles. While the building as a whole is large, an effective use of stratification allows the small points to be loosely linked to the larger whole, but without the vibrant points losing their sparkle.

However, the most difficult task was using roof tiles to create a screen to control the outside light. For the Xinjin Zhi Museum (2011) in Xinjin, south of Chengdu, which I had designed four years earlier, I had attached tiles one by one with vertical wires. Detailing with gaps between each of the tiles made the individual tiles feel as much as possible like points, but in Hangzhou I wanted to take a further step. If the wires crisscrossed at 45-degree angles and tiles were attached individually at the intersections, the tiles ought to feel more scattered and vibrant as points.

The key to this was that the tiles were not placed upright, as in Xinjin, but horizontally so that the edge of each tile was visible. With their sharply delineated cross-sections visible, the tiles were closer to being points. A different method was also used to attach the tiles, in which the protruding tiles were unevenly arrayed. This further strengthened the impression of a random accumulation of small, independent points, which formed a single hazy or cloud-like screen.

The fact that the tiles that were used are inconsistent, soiled, damaged and uneven indicates that the points have freedom; that each point is more point-like. If we want to liberate points more fully, we must therefore embrace dirt and relish damage.

This is all about designing buildings that are open to the long, uncertain period of time that follows after they are completed. Even if a building is soiled or damaged in various ways after it is completed, the points – which have been disparate from the start – will tolerate and accept the ageing process, whereas structures that are too clean and orderly do not. Contemporary Japanese architecture has evolved towards intolerance, and as a result, Japanese cities have become overly sterile and unwelcoming environments that are seemingly ruined by even minor soiling or damage.

Just as Wassily Kandinsky noted that lithographs can be modified indefinitely and are never 'finished', the architecture of disparate points is not confined to the limited time-frame of the building's completion. It has a tolerance of dirt and damage hard-wired into it from the start and, like a lithograph, is open to unlimited time stretching on to eternity.

TRIANGLES AS VERSATILE POINTS

In applying polygon division to the terrain at the Chengdu Museum, triangles were used as units rather than quadrilaterals. Any complex surface can be approximated as an aggregation of triangles, so in this sense, a quadrilateral is always just a plane, but a triangle is both a plane and an entity with the freedom of a point. Quadrilaterals are confined; triangles are at liberty.

Buildings are usually constructed with quadrilaterals as basic units, and this is true whether we look at plan views or elevation views. However, several architects recognized the inflexibility of the quadrilateral. Frank Lloyd Wright (1867–1959), who based his designs on natural principles, experimented with various forms and focused on the possibilities of the triangle. Buckminster Fuller (1895–1983) and Louis Kahn (1901–1974), who were influenced by Wright, also had a strong interest in triangles.[35]

Underlying the ideas of all three was the philosophical movement known as Transcendentalism, which emerged in 19th-century America, just before the country's industrialization. Transcendentalism involved a reverence for nature and a pursuit of harmony between nature and the human spirit that led to the geometry of the triangle. In religious terms their ideas were close to those of Unitarianism, and both Transcendentalists and Unitarians thoroughly rejected Calvinism, a Protestant denomination that emphasized a life of toil and asceticism.

In contrast to this, Le Corbusier and other architects who led the European Modernist movement were much closer

in spirit to Calvinism; La Chaux-de-Fonds, the city in the mountains of Switzerland where Le Corbusier was born, is said to be where Calvinists from the south of France ended up after fleeing persecution.

In *The Protestant Ethic and the Spirit of Capitalism* (1905), Max Weber notes the contributions of Calvinist asceticism to modern capitalism. He also makes frequent references to the fact that Calvinism's adherents favoured large glass windows and endeavoured not to hide anything from God, suggesting a connection to the large glass windows of Modernism.

So, at one extreme we have Calvinism, modern capitalism and the huge glass quadrilaterals of Modernism, while the opposing extreme sees Transcendentalism's critique of capitalism, embrace of life in the woods and affinity for the triangle.

Wright said: 'In pattern-based design, the triangle is my aspiration, the square is integrity, and the circle represents infinity. When these forms become three-dimensional, architectural inspiration strikes and they become my playground.' (Frank Lloyd Wright, *A Testament*, 1957.)

The origin of his interest in the triangle is often attributed to a set of building blocks that were given to him by his mother. Designed by the German educator, Friedrich Fröbel (1782–1852), the blocks went beyond simple cubes and rectangles to include other polygons and spheres. Demonstrating just how important this was to his development, Wright is quoted as saying: 'For several years I sat at the little kindergarten table-top… and played… with the cube, the sphere and the triangle – these smooth wooden maple blocks… All are in my fingers to this day.' (George Hersey, *Architecture and Geometry in the Age of the Baroque*, 2002.)

TSUMIKI: AN EXPANDABLE SYSTEM MODELLED ON PINE BRANCHES

Triangles played an important role in Fröbel's toys, and I have also designed unique building blocks composed entirely of triangles. In 2016 I was asked by More Trees, a non-profit forest conservancy organization founded by the musician Ryuichi Sakamoto, to design a new type of building block made with Japanese wood. As a rule, conventional building blocks are cubic or rectangular. They are a translation of the traditional Western building construction method of masonry – in which stones and bricks are stacked – into toy form, and structures built with them are inevitably heavy and brittle. My goal was to fundamentally shift the paradigm and create lighter and more see-through building blocks that were appropriate for fostering the growth of children in the current era.

36 Examples of the structures that can be built out of TSUMIKI.

The resulting building system, called TSUMIKI (literally, 'stacking wood', the word for building blocks in Japanese), consists of triangular units made from beautiful Miyazaki cedar.[36] However, TSUMIKI were not made simply by turning rectangular blocks into triangular ones. Unlike some of Fröbel's blocks, which are triangular, but thoroughly solid blocks that cannot be stacked up to create something light with a sense of transparency, TSUMIKI were made of cedar only 7 mm ($^{28}/_{100}$ in.) thick and shaped like forking pine branches. In this way they are not for 'building' (or 'stacking') in the conventional sense, but for 'assembling' or 'interconnecting'.

To encourage the act of assembling, triangular notches were cut into the ends of the boards, so the pine-branch-form units can not only be stacked upwards, but can also be assembled and interconnected in various directions. In other words, TSUMIKI not only produces see-through structures, but also steers clear of the dull action of 'stacking'. I wanted children to experience the joy and delight of assembling and interconnecting, without the formality of masonry that underlies the Western architectural tradition; assembling and interconnecting are much freer acts, which allow the mind and body a wider range of activity.

Consequently, the points (units) of TSUMIKI do not form dull, heavy masses but remain light and independent. These free, friendly points can be connected in any direction, and were made possible by the incorporation of linear elements into points, in much the same way that the Water Branch was created by incorporating linear elements into the masonry-style point of the Water Block. However, the introduction of the triangle principle gave TSUMIKI a lightness that the Water Branch does not possess. This is because it is not a closed triangle, but a forking form like the boughs of a pine tree. In this sense, TSUMIKI is actually more branch-like than the Water Branch, and more open as a system.

Branch-like forking structures can often be found in nature, be it at the microscopic scale of cells, in tree branches or in massive landforms. Wright cited nature in pointing to the essentiality of triangles, but I prefer to call the forms 'branches' (or 'pine branches') rather than triangles, as I believe this gives a deeper understanding of the principles behind the form. Branching is not only a connecting principle, but also a fundamental principle in the growth and change of organisms. Thus, the essence of nature is concealed within the triangles of branches.

CHECKERBOARD PATTERNS AS POINTS

I have made various attempts to lift stone out of the realm of volume: the Stone Museum took on the challenge of a porous masonry structure, and the Stone Card Castle succeeded in thinning stone until it became linear. However, in neither one of them was stone scattered enough to be described as points.

Lotus House (2005)[37] was my first project to bring stones fully into the point realm. A client commissioned a villa in the woods of Hayama, Japan, and while this particular client does not usually intervene in the plans and designs, this time they insisted on building the villa with Roman stone known as travertine. The most renowned travertine comes from quarries at Tivoli, near Rome, and it was used in many ancient Roman buildings, including the Papal Basilica of Saint Peter (St Peter's Basilica) and other buildings in the Vatican. A well-known example from the 20th century is Ludwig Mies van der Rohe's use of the stone for the base of the Barcelona Pavilion, a modernist masterpiece.

Travertine is a porous stone with numerous tiny holes, but while the texture is pleasant, stone can easily form heavy volumes. So how could this tricky material be transformed into something light?

I started thinking about detailing in the form of light screens of thinly sliced stone, which would allow both light and air to pass through. At first I tried a striped pattern, but somehow it did not feel weightless enough. Several striped screen prototypes were made with thin wooden slats, but while it was light enough when using wood, when a screen

37 Lotus House /2005 . Hayama. Japan. Thinly sliced travertine is arranged in a staggered pattern.

was made with stone cut to the same dimensions, it instantly gained weight and lost lightness and transparency.

In architecture, it is common for a design to have the shape and dimensions, but to be thoroughly transformed as soon as the material is changed. Even when lines or points have the same shapes, they become something else entirely when made with different materials.

At this point, I shifted gears and tried mounting thin stones in a checkerboard pattern instead of stripes. When a full-scale sample of the wall was fabricated, it was found that although the aperture ratio was the same (50 per cent of the wall), it had a completely different feel to a striped pattern with a 50 per cent aperture ratio. A light, airy, translucent screen emerged, and the light points of travertine seemed to flutter in the air like flower petals. That was when I decided to call this house Lotus House. The lotus blossoms planted in the pond in front of the house and the stone petals of travertine seemed to be singing together in harmony.

This checkerboard pattern also appears on the exterior wall of Nagaoka City Hall (2012). In response to citizens' requests for a plaza where people could gather even during winter, the government offices and arena are arranged around a covered plaza, which I call the inner *doma* (a hard-packed earthen-floored space in traditional Japanese interiors). It was designed in consultation with residents, with the intention of creating a new type of public space that was not a hard, formal, stone-paved European-style plaza. The floors of *doma* in Japanese farmhouses always consist of *tataki*, a mixture of earth and lime that is beaten down into a warm, slightly damp and uniquely textured surface.

Choosing a suitable material for the walls surrounding the inner *doma* was an easy choice: it shouldn't be concrete, stone or aluminium, but high-quality Echigo cedar that could be sourced from the mountains nearby. However, a city hall is not a residential building, and the walls went up to a height of approximately 20 metres (65 feet). If such large walls were covered completely with wood, the result would be bland, flat and at the same time claustrophobic. Up close, wood looks like a living thing with its grain and colour variations, but there was a danger that when standing in the large courtyard and looking up at the high walls, people would only see heavy, dull, brown walls.

To make the wood feel like wood – even from a distance – we fabricated panel-units consisting of several boards, and then arranged these units in a checkerboard pattern. Now, rather than continuous planes of wood, there were scattered, floating wooden points. The panels were attached to the wall at different, alternating angles, producing a zigzag effect that enhanced the points' sensation of lightness.

The most difficult aspect of this was determining the optimum sizes of the panels (points). If the points were too small in relation to the overall space, their presence as points would disappear, and the panels would revert to being a bland, flat surface. On the other hand, if the points were too large, each would assert itself too strongly and the space as a whole would lose its lightness. Only when points of the right size were scattered around the space would their inherent lightness and transparency emerge.

RAILWAY GRAVEL AS FREE POINTS

I derived significant insights into the sizes of points from a study on the dimensions of gravel under railroad ties.[38] The layering of rails, railroad ties and gravel distributes the load of the train car body and prevents it from damaging the soft soil below. On railways, the load is dispersed initially by the yielding of the linear iron rails, which transfers force to the linear ties; the load on the ties is then dispersed by the gravel beneath them. This multi-layered force distribution ensures that the ground beneath the railway line will not be hollowed out or ruptured.

A key point here is that the gravel is not bound together with adhesive, but each point is able to move and shift. The entire mound of gravel acts as a cushion because the gravel consists of free rather than constrained points, and it is the size of individual pieces of gravel that guarantees this freedom. If sand were spread under the ties, instead of gravel, the aggregation of these too-small points would not be able to distribute the force and the load would be concentrated, damaging the ground.

This offers an insight into the relationships between natural and built structures. Various points and lines intervene between the natural environment (the ground) and the

38 Railway tracks. Hamburg. Germany.

people riding in railway cars, enabling the two to connect
smoothly. Architecture, likewise, must smoothly connect
nature and humankind.

Gravel is the ideal material for spreading under railroad
ties, but could this seemingly free-moving and disorganized
material that is actually acting as a magnificent cushion, also
serve as a model for architecture that connects the natural
and human worlds? Our small and fragile bodies should be
connected to something larger, like the natural world, not
through the medium of something stiff and unyielding like
concrete, but through the medium of diverse particles. If
there is such a thing as democratic architecture, I believe
it is like the gravel on a railroad track, with the same
versatility and flexibility.

CHECKERBOARD PATTERNS AND FRUGALITY

When the checkerboard pattern wall of Nagaoka City Hall was completed, a local historian told an interesting story. The Nagaoka Domain (in present-day Niigata Prefecture) was known for its austerity and fortitude, and there was no indulgence in luxury. When Nagaoka Castle burnt to the ground during the Boshin War, the Mineyama Domain sent 100 bales of rice as a sympathy gift. However, the Nagaoka clan famously sold them and used the money to educate their children.

In keeping with the Nagaoka Domain's spirit of stoic simplicity, its castle's sliding doors were covered with small pieces of paper pasted together in checkerboard formation, rather than being decorated with large paintings. This meant that if a sheet of paper was soiled or damaged, only that single sheet needed to be replaced, whereas just a small stain in the corner of a large picture or design might require the entire sliding door to be replaced.

The checkerboard is closely connected to the spirit of frugality, and this is true of the checkerboard-like wooden wall that we designed for Nagaoka City Hall.[39] Compared to an entire wall covered with wood, only half the amount of wood is needed for a checkerboard pattern, and if any of that wood becomes stained or discoloured over time, it can be replaced one unit at a time, just like the decoration on Nagaoka Castle's sliding doors. Used in this way, scattered points are an excellent means of achieving frugality and economy, and points in general make for highly sustainable and flexible designs.

39 Nagaoka City Hall Aore 2012 . Japan. We arranged panels made of cedar plank staggered with slightly differentiated angles.

DISPERSAL AND THE SAHARA DESERT

A state in which points are distributed and floating, as in a checkerboard, is sometimes called a 'dispersed state'. The term 'dispersed' was used originally in mathematics, but my mentor, the architect Hiroshi Hara (b. 1936), endeavoured to introduce it into the world of architecture.

Hara and his students at the University of Tokyo surveyed remote villages around the world, making drawings of their layouts and floor plans, and observing the rhythms of daily life, familial bonds and extraordinarily appealing and vibrant architecture that could potentially inspire designs for future cities and architecture. In his studies, Hara applied mathematical approaches to architecture, perhaps drawing inspiration from Claude Lévi-Strauss (1908–2009), who derived many insights from mathematics in his ethnographic research.

When I was a student, Professor Hara and I spent two months together in the winter of 1978, travelling in a Jeep, researching settlements in and around the Sahara

40 Aerial view of Ait Benhaddou, Morocco.

Desert in West Africa. During the trip, Hara often used the word 'dispersed'.

Villages in and around the Sahara are characterized by compound dwellings, in which huts are clustered together with spaces between them.[40] Polygamy is common in the region, and a husband often visits one wife's hut per day, dines at that hut and stays overnight with his wife and children. Hara described this format, in which the huts of wives are loosely clustered around a courtyard, as a 'dispersed community'.

A state in which points are loosely and chaotically aggregated, with distance between them, is a dispersed state, while its opposite is a state in which points are closely interconnected with no space between them. As we travelled in the desert, we discussed the idea that the dispersed state is optimal for human relations, and that the state of ultimate concentration, in which all points are closely connected, is fascism. We spoke, over a fire in the desert, about how the architecture of the future must aim for dispersal, like the compounds of the Sahara.

Admiration for dispersed states – in other words, a keen interest in points – grew within me during this trip to the Sahara. When I began to think about architecture in terms of the mathematical concept of the discrete, I realized that mathematics and quantum mechanics were powerful weapons to have in my arsenal. Discrete mathematics is an important field in modern mathematics, and it has taught me that we can see new aspects of the world when we view it as a scattered array of particles, rather than a continuum. Today, I believe that dispersal is not merely a concept related to planar layout, but one that can be applied to all areas of architecture, both in terms of materials and detailing.

LINE

THE VOLUMES OF LE CORBUSIER AND MIES

The history of 20th-century architecture can be seen as a story of conflict between volume and line. Early in the century, two masters revolutionized the architectural world and subsequently spearheaded modernist architecture: Le Corbusier and Mies van der Rohe, who embodied volume and line respectively and illustrated the two opposite poles of design in the era.

The most efficient solution for quickly and inexpensively achieving the massive volumes demanded by the exploding populations and booming economies of the time was a three-dimensional lattice that combined columns and beams (vertical and horizontal lines). In place of traditional masonry, which entailed carefully laying small points of stone or brick one by one, line-based construction – the assembly of columns and beams – became the default approach to building in the modern world from the 20th century onwards.

Reacting against the classical architecture that had dominated Europe until the 20th century – architecture that since ancient Greek and Roman times had been based on lines in the form of columns ('orders') – Le Corbusier was led away from line and towards volume. In *Towards an Architecture* (1933) he confessed his passion for volumes by defining architecture as 'the masterly, correct and magnificent play of masses [i.e. volumes] brought together in light'.

If the 20th century needed colossal volumes, it was Le Corbusier's straightforward strategy to realize those volumes in concrete. As soon as architecture is defined in

41 Palace of Assembly. Chandigarh. 2006.

terms of volumes it becomes liberated at best, or brutal at worst. Le Corbusier had thorough knowledge of the characteristics of volumes and used them to their fullest, unafraid of embracing brutality when necessary.

Le Corbusier's attitude towards volume became even more radical in his later years. Eventually, he sublimated all architecture into 'an art of volume', as in Notre-Dame du Haut (1955), and his urban plan for the city of Chandigarh, India.[41] Indeed, when he was shown around the Katsura Imperial Villa in Kyoto, he dismissively muttered 'Too many lines', a natural reaction for a partisan of volumes when encountering overwhelmingly linear architecture.

In comparison, when Bruno Taut (1880–1938), one of the best-known German Expressionist architects, was given a tour of the same villa on May 4, 1933 – which happened to be his birthday – he was moved to tears and later wrote that it was the best birthday of his life.

Taut, who never gained the same degree of recognition as Le Corbusier or Mies, almost seemed to turn his back on the 20th century altogether. He rejected the volumes of concrete and the stark lines of steel frames, and was instead enchanted by the wooden lines of the villa, delicate to the point of fragility. This reflects his sensitivity and vulnerability as a human being and as an architect.

The Hyuga Villa in Atami is his only extant residential work in Japan, and is replete with the slender lines he favoured. The walls are of thin, interlaced bamboo, with unusual light fixtures woven with bamboo. However, Japanese people at that time admired American-style steel-frame construction and did not understand Taut's delicate lines; the architect left Japan despondent.

Mies also eschewed volume in favour of line, but he was not a romantic like Taut, and dedicated himself to the pursuit of clean, pure lines through metal − a thoroughly modern material. Metal lines recur throughout the structures he designed, concealing the gigantic volumes of the skyscrapers demanded by the 20th century and causing them to blend into the sky.

Mies was such an illustrious figure in pre-war Germany that he served as principal of the Bauhaus, but he was later forced to flee the Nazis and emigrated to the US in 1938. After World War II he had the option of returning home to Germany, but chose to remain in the US. They needed each other: the US at the time was calling for massive volumes composed of lines, and Mies was pursuing an aesthetic of line that could only be realized through American industrial might. In this sense, the 20th century was decidedly 'the American century' for Mies, while Le Corbusier stayed in Europe and continued to reject the American way.

It is not that Le Corbusier was uninterested in skyscrapers – he repeatedly produced urban plans in which skyscrapers proliferated to an assaultive degree, such as Contemporary City for Three Million Inhabitants (1922), Plan Voisin (1925) and Radiant City (1950). In fact, Le Corbusier earnestly aspired to design skyscrapers, but French intellectuals of the time derided his plans to demolish Paris and replace it with soaring superblocks.

To the eyes of the French, these visions may have looked like the pipe dreams of an eccentric from the Swiss countryside longing for American-style heroic scale, but Le Corbusier wrote in *When the Cathedrals Were White* (1937) that 'the skyscrapers of New York are too small and there are too many of them'. Le Corbusier certainly admired enormous volumes, but he dismissed Mies-style devices, such as concealing these volumes with uniform lines of mass-produced metal. Ultimately, Le Corbusier never realized a skyscraper in France, nor did he find acceptance in the US.

Instead, he went to India, a country that stood in stark contrast to both France and the US. Starting in 1951, he was engaged in the planning of Chandigarh, a new provincial capital, and visited scorching-hot India a total of 23 times, despite his advanced age. India was a place where an American-style use of lines to compose and cosmetically conceal volumes was completely invalid. The technology to produce such straight lines simply did not exist in India at the time, and there was no choice but to place rough concrete volumes directly on the country's sandy red soil.

His challenging project was not only a major milestone for him personally, but also had a profound impact on subsequent architectural design worldwide, as Chandigarh sowed the seeds of the raw concrete aesthetic that would come to be known as Brutalism. Brutalism was highly influential in post-war Japan, and rough concrete poured into tight-grained cedar-plank formwork became the official uniform of post-war Japanese public buildings.

I believe Le Corbusier had a greater impact on the 20th century in his later years than in the early part of his career, which was exemplified by the elegant geometry of his white cubic Villa Savoye. In Chandigarh, Le Corbusier demonstrated that structures could be built on the roughest terrain and that modern people could live robustly and vibrantly in these environments. It was an architecture of hope that was applicable to all parts of the world, in stark contrast to Mies's exaltation of America.

Early in his career Le Corbusier was a leading figure in modernist architecture, which was the international aesthetic of an industrialized society that sought to standardize the world. By contrast, his later work pointed in the direction of diversification and gave people all over the world something to aspire to. It was not an international, but a global architecture. I have often criticized Le Corbusier's signature concrete style, but post-Chandigarh Le Corbusier has influenced me in many ways. There is something in Chandigarh that transcends the points, lines and planes of the 20th century.

KENZŌ TANGE'S UNALIGNED LINES

Kenzō Tange (1913–2005) was a Japanese architect who explored diverse approaches that were radically different to Le Corbusier's work at Chandigarh. He also endeavoured to look beyond an American-style, industrialized mode of linear architecture, with methodologies that diverged from those of Mies.

Tange's inspiration came from traditional Japanese architecture, and in the Kagawa Prefectural Government Office (1958), he translated the displaced points of contact of traditional Japanese wooden structures into concrete. In traditional Japanese wood-frame construction, lines are often shifted or unaligned, so that one linear element is gently placed on top of another. With this slight displacement there is no need to notch the wood and lose any of its cross-sectional area, making it possible to maintain the full strength of the linear elements.

This interweaving of lines differed from the Western Cartesian grid, in which multiple lines intersect at single points, and Japanese carpenters knew that by intentionally not aligning the points of contact, lines could be made lighter and freer, creating movement in space. They were also well aware that this displacement of linear elements would enable lines to remain lines, instead of becoming planes, creating a sense of lightness and transparency.

Tange also understood the effect of displaced lines, and with the Kagawa Prefectural Government Office he shifted the points of contact of concrete columns and beams so they did not intersect at a single point. In this way, he demonstrated that concrete could be used to create light, independent, appealing lines that were not buried within a blocky volume.

Tange subsequently designed the Yoyogi National Gymnasium[42] for the 1964 Tokyo Olympics, in which two massive vertical concrete lines (columns) shoot up from the earth to the sky, with steel cables suspended from them. The lines of the cables are much thinner than the lines of

42 Yoyogi National Gymnasium in Shibuya. designed by architect Kenzo Tange for the 1964 Summer Olympic Games. Tokyo. Japan.

the concrete, and curve elegantly with the force of gravity for stunning effect.

Swiftly gaining global recognition, Tange's work was the first to describe the kind of subtle and graceful lines that were thought to be unachievable with concrete. It also differed from the straight lines embodying American industrial might that Mies applied to skyscrapers. With the bold inclusion of flexible steel cables – which had only been used for civil engineering projects, such as suspension bridges – Tange introduced free and seemingly organic lines into 20th-century architecture.

The Yoyogi National Gymnasium also turned a new page in the history of the Japanese roof. To that point, the roof was often a flat surface, but Tange utilized thin, delicate cables that branched off from a main cable running across a beam between two columns, so the roof was given new life as an aggregation of lines.

There have been several major turning points in the history of the Japanese roof. Ancient and pre-modern times, were characterized by thatched roofs, which appeared to be volumes, but were actually aggregations of fine lines, namely the stalks of tall grasses. Even after the introduction of roof tiles in the Edo Period, the technique of alternating convex and concave tiles – known as *hongawara* – was still used to produce aggregations of lines, and the Japanese roof retained its charm as a linear aggregation by emphasizing the lines generated by the upper convex tiles.

However, the invention of *sangawara* (also known as *kanryaku-gawara* or 'simplified roof tiles') saw the convex *marugawara* and concave *hiragawara* incorporated into a single tile. Along with flat roofs imported from the West, this saw the beauty of line disappear from the Japanese roof, although Tange succeeded in resurrecting its linear character for the Olympic Games.

FROM LINE TO VOLUME: THE DEGRADATION OF JAPANESE ARCHITECTURE

When the Olympic Games were over, lines faded once more from Japanese architecture. Not all structural issues could be solved with cables, and while the bronze lines of Mies were expensive, a cable-suspended roof was more expensive still. Tange's graceful curves may have been feasible for the Olympic Games – the event of the century – but once the party was over, Japanese architecture shifted from an architecture of line to an architecture of volume. As things returned to business as usual, 'ordinary solutions' suited to 'ordinary buildings' were called for, in terms of both cost and programme.

In Tokyo, as well as other cities and towns throughout Japan, society demanded that large numbers of 'ordinary buildings' were built during the period of rapid economic growth. The 'construction state' – a system designed to lubricate the gears of the economy and politics by erecting structures – truly came into its own, propelled by a massive influx of taxpayer funds that were spent without hesitation.

However, for this system to continue running smoothly, humdrum buildings still needed to be given a strong identity so they would not just blend into the surroundings. They needed a distinct character that justified the vast amounts of public money being spent on them, and to this end, these run-of-the-mill buildings – no more than aggregations of volumes – were designed to stand out.

Rather than acrobatic dances of lines, as in the Yoyogi National Gymnasium, more pragmatic and systematic designs were employed to give buildings an identity. It was two of Kenzō Tange's pupils – Arata Isozaki and Kisho Kurokawa (1934–2007) – who responded precisely to this social need. Although both were known as artists with strong personalities, and not merely pragmatic or systematic designers, a dispassionate analysis of their work reveals they were architects of volume, not of line. They made great use of geometry to arrange heavy concrete masses, imbuing them with strong character and identity.

For his part, Isozaki used cubes to organize and govern the conventional format of *hakomono* ('box structures'; a term usually used to refer to public buildings), producing unconventional, monumental works.[43] The cube is a central motif of European Classicist architecture in the Greco-Roman tradition, and European architects used the Platonic geometry of the Greek tradition to transform what tended to be dull masonry structures into luminous monuments.

43 The Museum of Modern Art. Gunma. Japan. designed by architect Atara Isozaki.

Isozaki used this powerful tool – Western in origin – to derive symbolic monumental structures from what could easily have been plodding masses of concrete.

Meanwhile, Kurokawa began competing with Isozaki using the geometric form of the cone, which similarly gave his volumes a distinct identity. Isozaki- and Kurokawa-style volumes, governed by the Platonic solids, quickly became the model for Japan's architects, architectural design firms and construction contractors' design departments, as Platonic volumes were the easiest to imitate, and the most cost-effective, systematic method.

Buildings constructed in this manner were often derided as *hakomono*, an apt description that captures the essence of the volumetric method and alludes to the architecture's complicity with the social, political and economic establishment of the boom era. Post-Tange, Japanese contemporary architecture abandoned lines, degenerated into volumes and embraced the ease of a mass-production system.

STARTING OUT IN A WOODEN HUT

When I began studying architecture in the late 1970s, the era of *hakomono* was at its peak, and Isozaki and Kurokawa stood as the leaders and propagandists of this trend. They became stars of the architectural world, legitimizing *hakomono* with their brilliant discourse.

Personally, however, I was drawn to Professor Yoshichika Uchida, who was exploring new possibilities in wooden architecture, and Professor Hara Hiroshi, who was known for his research on rural villages. I decided to study under them because I felt fundamentally uncomfortable with the heavy, closed volumes of concrete. By comparison, the wood-frame Japanese structures described by Uchida and the villages that fascinated Hara were both foreign objects, strangers to the age of volume. They appeared to be aggregations of chaotic lines – anarchic outside agents that were the furthest and most liberated from the *hakomono* style.

I was born and raised in a small wooden house that was built by my maternal grandfather just before the war. My grandfather, a doctor in Oi, had originally built this small, crude wooden hut in Okurayama on the Tokyu Toyoko Line – where one was surrounded by rice paddies and fields as soon as one got off the train – as a shed for his only hobby, gardening. The rooms were floored with tatami mats, and separated by sliding doors, rather than walls; draughts from the wooden sashes made the interior chilly. This was not stylish 'traditional Japanese architecture', but a hut built of wood, earth and paper. The earth-plastered walls were full of cracks that continually shed dust on the tatami mats, and

44 Rural mountain village in Japan. 1880s.

only the earthen-floored area at the entrance was extra-ordinarily large.[44]

This hut instilled in me a sense of intimate scale and of see-through spaces, and when I looked at the reality around me, the blocky concrete *hakomono* that have been the standard in Japan since 1964 seemed unbearably heavy and intimidating. This discomfort became even stronger when I enrolled in the architecture department at university: the curriculum of the time continued to exalt the modernist architecture of Le Corbusier and Mies, which was nothing but a painful ordeal for me.

THE LINES OF GAUDI

In the winter of 1978, I joined Professor Hiroshi Hara and a group of pupils on a two-month trip to survey villages in Africa. We shipped two four-wheel-drive vehicles by sea, but as the Mediterranean Sea in winter is subject to strong monsoon winds from the south, known as *sirocco*, the container ship could only get as far as the port of Barcelona in Spain.

Thanks to this wind, I was able to visit Barcelona and see the work of Antoni Gaudí (1852–1926) in person for the first time. Seeing the real thing, rather than photographs, changed my impression of Gaudí. Designs such as Park Güell – a heavy mass of concrete covered with randomly broken tiles – had made a powerful impression, but led me to see him as an architect of volumes and thus to steer clear of him.

However, in person, I could see that Gaudí's work was overflowing with thin, delicate lines, with the cast-iron moulding being especially beautiful – the fact that his father was a coppersmith made perfect sense. This metal detailing was so refined that it shattered my image of Gaudí as an artist of concrete and tile.

Most interesting of all was a transparent screen modelled on palm fronds, with its keen and slender lines. Gaudí intuitively understood that the structures of plants underlie the principle of lines:[45] plants suck up water from the ground by means of lines (their roots and veins) and transport it to their leaves. Plants are aggregations of lines, which support and sustain their bodies. Architects of the late 19th and early

45 La Sagrada Família. Barcelona. Spain.

20th century, from Art Nouveau to Gaudí, were thus fascinated by plants and developed an architecture of fine lines rather than of stone, brick and volume.

However, from Mies onwards, these vegetation-inspired lines were lost and replaced by the straight lines of American industry. Perhaps what I am trying to do is revert from the lines of industry to the lines of plants. The delicate turn-of-the-century lines of Gaudí and Art Nouveau acted as a kind of critique of the Industrial Revolution and the linearity of 19th-century industry, but these lines were extremely short-lived, soon to be overwhelmed and erased by the new lines of 20th-century industry.

POINTILLISM

From Barcelona we drove to Marseille, where we took a ferry to the port of Algiers in Algeria, before heading inland and staying in the city of Ghardaïa, which Le Corbusier apparently loved. From a distance, it looked more like a low hill than a town, but as we drew closer, we found that an aggregation of small white box structures had been piled up into a single hill-like mass. A long process of constructing small white boxes on top of a pre-existing hill had generated an organic settlement, somewhere between natural terrain and a human-made artefact. The community struck me as a pointillist rendering of a landform: if each dwelling in a settlement is a small unit, the natural result is pointillism.

Pointillism emerged when artists endeavoured to get at the essence of nature. The Post-Impressionist painter Georges Seurat (1859–1891)[46] is said to have discovered the pointillist method when he was attempting to render the sea off Normandy and Brittany. Unlike mountains, which have forms that can be depicted, the sea consists of constantly changing textures, and Seurat determined that the essence of the sea lies in a state of constantly flickering points, thus arriving at pointillism.

Seurat's method is similar to what I am trying to do in architecture: to liberate architecture from form and release it into a world of flickering light, like the sea off the coast of Normandy and Brittany. Indeed, the architect Greg Lynn (b. 1964), a pioneer of computational design (also known as parametric design), once described my work as an architecture of pointillism. As the basis of digital technology is

46 Georges Seurat. *A Sunday on La Grande Jatte*. 1884–86. Oil on canvas. 207.5 308.1 cm 81 ³⁄₄ 121 ¹⁄₄ in.

approximation through minuscule points, it is unsurprising that Lynn would take an interest in pointillism. However, well before the 1990s – when computational design became a hot topic – it was Ghardaïa that first awakened me to computational pointillism.

From Ghardaïa, we continued southwards through the Sahara Desert. After the desert comes the savannah – vast tropical grasslands that stretch between the desert and the rainforest. The desert is only for passing through, and is not fit for human habitation. But once we had reached the savannah we began seeing signs of people and came across one settlement after another, enabling us to begin our survey of villages in earnest.

These villages consisted of small huts dotting the plains, grouped into compounds that housed extended families. As an individual unit, each hut was very small, and these points were scattered across the savannah. As I mentioned in the previous chapter, Hara described this format as 'dispersed', and it opened my eyes to the intriguing world of points.

Compounds on the savannah are essentially aggregations of small, self-enclosed boxes constructed from sun-dried bricks. Their layouts are certainly interesting, but when viewed from close up at ground level, the huts themselves are closed, heavy volumes. What I thought to be points from a distance revealed themselves to be only volumes.

THE LINES OF THE TROPICAL RAINFOREST

Beyond the savannah lies the rainforest. Here, plants become the materials for constructing dwellings, and architecture becomes lighter and more transparent.[47] One leaves the world of volume and enters the world of line. Moreover, each line is much thinner than the steel or aluminium we are used to seeing in our everyday surroundings. Because the lines consist of tree branches, vines and palm fronds, their thinness is only natural; the rainforest was a world of lines finer and more delicate than the 10 cm (4 in.) square lumber I knew from my childhood house in Okurayama.

When I saw these lines, thinner than any I had encountered before, the layout, form and design of the village faded from my view and seemed unimportant. This sensation was as pleasant as dozing off in a hammock woven from plant fibres, savouring the breeze and dappled shade. It reminded me of when I was a child and my mother hung *kaya* (Japanese nutmeg-yew) screens at night. These woven plant-fibre screens were to repel mosquitoes, and the scent and texture of the vegetation made the moment when I bedded down inside this netting a blissful one. These are some of my happiest childhood memories.

47 Traditional Ryukyu village in Naha. Okinawa. Japan.

People living in the rainforest looked happy too, surrounded by those slender lines of vegetation, no matter how chaotic and uneven the lines might be. My rainforest experience introduced me to a new world of lines, and the trip to Africa provided crucial inspiration for reviving this architecture, which had been discarded under the leadership of Isozaki, Kurokawa and others during the construction boom of the rapid growth period.

However, the leader of our mission, Professor Hara, showed little interest in rainforest dwellings. He may have felt they lacked what interested him most: mathematics. For me, the rainforest felt like a treasure trove of mathematics. Hara – a member of roughly the same generation as Isozaki and Kurokawa – was not interested in cluttered plant-fibre structures rife with extraneous elements. I was struck by the unwelcome thought that Hara, too, had not escaped his generation's fate: to build blocky, concrete structures.

THE LINES OF MODERNISM AND THE
LINES OF JAPANESE ARCHITECTURE

It may be that Arata Isozaki, Kisho Kurokawa and Hiroshi Hara's generation abandoned line because the only lines they knew were the ungainly ones of modernist architecture, which used lines to slice through the heft of stone and brick masonry structures.[48] Assembling frames from lines of concrete and steel created permeable and expandable frame systems, and the essence of modernism lay in the efficient expansion of volume through the use of such frames; they were the optimal solution for the 20th century, when the primary objective was the expansion of space.

A basic principle of modernism was to construct frames by building columns and beams of concrete and steel, and both on paper and in practice, the 20th century was constrained by an inability to break out of the frame. The most efficient spacing between columns was around 10 m (33 ft.) and, if the material was concrete, the columns should be about 1 m (3.3 ft.) square. As the height of beams was also about 1 m, the bulky 1-m square became the standard size for modernist architecture, and sturdy frames made it possible to create a 10-m square space without columns.

These abstract, 10-m square spaces suited the needs of the times, and objects and people were able to move freely within them. Freedom of movement within a column-free space is the vision of Newtonian mechanics, in which objects move in empty, abstract space according to the laws of motion. Architecture is always behind the curve, but it

48 Kyoto Station in Kyoto. Japan. designed by Hiroshi Hara.

finally caught up with Newtonian mechanics in the 20th century, centuries after the fact.

However, while Modernist architecture had finally caught up with Newton, its frames of thick columns and beams seemed to me like concrete prisons. The grim frames that proliferated and covered cities around the world in the 20th century were altogether too hulking and dominant compared to the delicate and fragile human body. Human scale disappeared from homes and cities, and massive frames overpowered people as they lived in the shadow of Newton's centuries old, already mouldering dream.

By comparison, the lines that made up traditional Japanese wooden structures were far more delicate and less threatening to the human body. Both columns and beams had cross-sectional dimensions of 10 cm (4 in.) or less, and were only 3–4 m (10–13 feet) in length. Entire spaces were composed of gentle, delicate lines, as materials were small and light enough for one person to carry. Yet the technology and aesthetics needed to produce these beautiful lines was lying dormant in Japan.

DISPUTES OVER TRADITION AND THE ROBUST LINES OF THE JOMON PERIOD

Post-war Japanese modernism did not always lack interest in traditional Japanese architecture. The delicacy of the wood and steel frames of early post-war modernist architecture remains fresh even today. In Tange's case, the Kishi Memorial Gymnasium (1941),[49] from when he belonged to the office of Kunio Maekawa, and his own home in Seijo were ambitious attempts to approach the thin lines of traditional Japanese wooden structures. However, most Japanese architects forgot about fine lines and rushed to embrace bulky concrete frames instead.

Playing a role in this shift was a curious controversy known as the 'Jōmon dispute'. This dispute began with an assertion that the fine lines of early post-war modernism were soft, weak and reminiscent of the Yayoi Period (roughly 300 BCE–250 CE). Seiichi Shirai (1905–1983) and others of the Jōmon faction argued that Japan must recapture the strength of the preceding, prehistoric Jōmon Period, which saw the original emergence of Japanese culture. Tange's student, Isozaki, was heavily influenced by Shirai's Jōmon-like, volumetric designs, which were in stark contrast to those of his teacher.

The Jōmon faction was led by the artist Tarō Okamoto (1911–1996), who famously declared that 'art is an

49 Kishi Memorial Gymnasium in Shibuya. Tokyo. Japan.

explosion'. At Expo '70 in Osaka, Okamoto's robust lines –
in the form of his monumental sculpture, *Tower of the Sun*
– thrust up through the space frame of the Tange-designed
Festival Plaza. The resurgent Jōmon spirit shattered the
lines of Tange's 'Yayoi-style' space frame, which represented the pinnacle of Japan's steelmaking industry.

Okamoto's 'robust' monument perfectly symbolizes
the way vigorous lines propelled Japan's rapid economic
growth. This dispute over traditions was also a precursor to
the high-growth period of Japanese architecture, when the
emphasis shifted from line to volume.

In this economic boom time, only a small group were
pursuing fine lines in architecture. Isoya Yoshida (1894–
1974) and Togo Murano (1891–1984) were recognized as
standard-bearers of the traditional arts. They designed
high-end traditional restaurants and distinctive residences,
and occupied a zone outside the architectural mainstream

of Tange, Isozaki and Kurokawa. These 'refined masters' sought even finer lines using modern-day materials lines, which look surprisingly delicate, even today. Yoshida designed the equivalent of a bamboo blind using aluminium pipe, while Murano created a slim roof using a thin panel of aluminium in place of old-fashioned *hongawara* tiles.

While modernist architects like Tange were interested only in the silhouettes of volumes, Yoshida and Murano continued to grapple with the varieties of points, lines and planes that contemporary materials made possible. In this sense I believe they were truly cutting-edge, especially after Isozaki and Kurokawa reverted to box-based designs grounded in Western classicism, and yet the wisdom and accomplishments of Yoshida and Murano were largely ignored by the architectural world.

THE MOVABLE LINES OF JAPANESE WOOD-FRAME CONSTRUCTION

The lines of Japan's traditional wooden structures were not only thin, but also freely movable. This was a surprisingly futuristic approach. First of all, partitions composed of lines, such as sliding doors and *shoji* screens, could be moved at will in response to changes in daily circumstances. This system later ruled the office spaces of the 20th century, but the traditional precursor of the movable-partition system was actually much lighter and more sophisticated. Even more surprisingly, the columns themselves – the main structure supporting a building – could be moved freely, even after the building was completed.

The secret lay in the attics of Japanese buildings. Thanks to the insertion of a *wagoya* – a jungle-gym-like wooden

50 Interior roof structure of a traditional Japanese building dating from the Edo period.

roof truss[50] – between the ceiling and the roof, the slender columns that supported the roof and gave it firmness and rigidity could be shifted after completion. Remarkably, this system existed in Japan in the 14th century, and had no parallel anywhere else in the world.

Whereas the modernization of Western architecture involved the removal of walls and the creation of large spaces by means of massive column-and-beam frames, Japanese wood-frame construction used thin columns and beams to create flexible and modifiable spaces. As far back as the 14th century, Japan already had thin, delicate, movable lines instead of thick, immobile frames.

The traditional Japanese wooden system offers many suggestions for transcending the large, rigid spaces of 20th-century modernism, and the 'refined masters' also took up these movable lines in various ways. For example, Yoshida's Kitamura Residence (1965) allowed columns to be removed when changing the positions of the partitions, and the frames of fittings could also be moved or removed. When both columns and partition were removed, there was only an expanse of tatami mats left, as if the floor had always been empty. In Shin-Kiraku (1940), also designed by Yoshida, the huge partitions in the large hall could be shifted using electric motors.

CORE PRESSING AND SURFACE PRESSING

Another interesting aspect of traditional Japanese wood construction is that there were two approaches to dealing with line: core pressing (*shin-osae*), in which a linear element was treated as a centre line or 'core', and surface pressing (*men-osae*), in which a linear element was treated by its contours or outline. These two co-existed, with one or the other favoured depending on the situation.

Originally, Japanese carpenters used core pressing to draw blueprints, and as the basis for constructing buildings. This is because untreated logs or crooked beams were often used in private houses, and it was impossible to use contours when working with these 'still-living' lines.

In the *shinden-zukuri* style of aristocratic residences of the Heian Period (794–1185), floors were laid down with uncovered wooden planks. During the Kamakura Period (1185–1333), tatami mats were placed on the floor like furniture or cushions, and in the Muromachi Period (1336–1568) tatami mats were laid to cover the entire floor. Spreading these tatami mats in this way was a means of using small, limited spaces comfortably and effectively. However, when tatami mats are laid tightly to fill floors, the contours of surfaces become more important than their core: the mats need to be laid without gaps, so the area to be covered needs to be defined and limited.

This change in lifestyle led to a shift from core to surface pressing as the basis for architecture, as surface pressing was more practical and economical when it came to the efficient use of tatami flooring in limited spaces. In Kyoto-style tatami flooring, for example, each mat had a standard size of 3 × 6 *shaku* (approximately 1 × 2 m, or 3.3 × 6.6 feet). Securing these in place could therefore determine the position of columns, and with this method it was possible for people to take their mats with them when they moved.

However, Edo-style tatami flooring positioned the cores of pillars at a distance of 3, 6 and 9 *shaku*. Floors designed using these dimensions were then covered with tatami mats, although this meant the mats had irregular dimensions and people could not take them when they moved.

The Kyoto approach was urban and modern, while the Edo approach was rural and vernacular. However, the two methods of core and surface pressing co-existed and were skilfully used as appropriate to address the reality that linear elements and walls have a thickness. In both Edo and Kyoto, carpenters used core pressing and surface pressing depending on the section of the building they were working on, and today's Japanese carpenters can still respond flexibly to different situations using these two methods.

Meanwhile, in the West, the thickness of linear elements and walls remained a troublesome issue. Medieval archi-tects addressed it with a twin-column structure,[51] in which rows of arches were supported by paired columns, or groups of thin columns seemingly bound together. With multiple columns in a bundle, as found in the columns of Gothic churches, a grid system of repeating columns and an arch system supporting thick walls could co-exist.

51 Twin column structure in the cloister at Archbasilica of Saint John Lateran. Rome. Italy.

However, the most famous solution to this problem was the invention of twin columns by the early Renaissance architect, Filippo Brunelleschi. When columns are arranged in rows, there is always a breakdown at the internal corners, because both the columns and the walls have thickness, causing the rhythm of the columns to break down. The inevitable gap between abstract geometry conceived by the human brain and physical reality composed of matter is sometimes called the Brunelleschi problem. While Brunelleschi resolved this problem with the invention of twin columns – which remains a cutting-edge solution, even today – Japanese carpenters resolved the gap by using both core pressing and surface pressing.

THE FINE LINES OF HIROSHIGE

Can we ever regain the fine, shifting lines that were honed in traditional Japanese wooden structures over time? Can we introduce fine lines like those of grass enclosures in African rainforests? When fine lines are revived, what styles of architecture will emerge, what kinds of cities will be built and what sorts of relationships between humans and lines will be established?

My first attempt to grapple with line, with this issue in mind, was the Hiroshige Museum of Art (2000).[52] When I was asked to design a museum housing the work of the ukiyo-e artist Utagawa Hiroshige (1797–1858), I studied his works and saw how important lines were to him. In particular, I derived significant inspiration from one of his most iconic works: *Sudden Shower over Shin Ohashi Bridge and Atake* from the series *One Hundred Famous Views of Edo*.

The lines of *Sudden Shower…* also had a tremendous impact on two great artists who revolutionized their fields. One was Vincent van Gogh (1853–1890), the giant of Post-Impressionism, and the other was Frank Lloyd Wright, the American master of 20th-century modernist architecture who took the first steps in a movement towards architectural transparency.

Van Gogh made a copy of *Sudden Shower…* in oils, and cited Hiroshige as one of the artists he admired most, placing him in the same league as his Dutch compatriot Rembrandt, and his contemporary, Paul Cézanne. Van Gogh's praise for Hiroshige, ukiyo-e artist from an island nation far to the east, seemed altogether incongruous.

52 Washi wall at Nakagawa Machi Bato Hiroshige Museum of Art (2000), Japan.

Meanwhile, Wright wrote that he would not have arrived at his own architectural style without his encounters with two Japanese artists: Hiroshige and Tenshin Okakura. The series *One Hundred Famous Views of Edo*, which includes *Sudden Shower...*, was a particularly important body of work for Wright. He praised it in a 1950 lecture at Taliesin, describing it as 'the greatest landscape painting idea ever conceived. It is totally unique in the history of art.'

So, what made *Sudden Shower...* so appealing to these two artists? The secret lay in the lines of the rain. These two brilliant minds perceived Western painting up to the 19th century as being dominated by ponderous volumes, and sought to dismantle such volumes in their own work. After encountering the lines of Hiroshige, they made the Japanese artist an entry point into a new world of lightweight linearity.

Examining *Sudden Shower...* in detail, we see that the evening rain is depicted as lines, and bundles of these lines create a layer. The space is given three-dimensional depth through the superposition of thin layers, without using the perspective rendering on which European painting is based.

The basis of the perspective rendering method, which emerged in the Renaissance, is to depict objects close at hand as large, and objects far away as small, making it easy to convey three-dimensional depth in a two-dimensional image. By contrast, Hiroshige expressed spatial depth with a completely different technique.

In *Sudden Shower…* the bridge over the river does not grow narrower, despite receding into the distance, but is the same width on the far bank of the river as on the near bank. Meanwhile, the bridge girders are depicted as a see-through screen composed of fine lines, and the transparency generated by these lines conveys depth and the distance between the near and far sides of the river. It is possible to represent the bridge as a transparent screen because it is built of wood, and wooden structures and transparency are deeply and inseparably linked. It can be said that the wooden structure made use of the perspectival rendering method unnecessary.

Also noteworthy here is the substitution of the mathematical and abstract entity of straight lines for the natural phenomenon of rain. Art historians point out that this substitution is markedly East Asian and could not have occurred in traditional Western art. A basic premise of traditional Western art was that nature is an ambiguous, elusive and formless entity, an alien presence in stark contrast with the clean geometric forms of human-made objects. Western art was rooted in a view of the natural and the artificial being in opposition, with the latter hierarchically above the former.

The 'discovery of nature' in Western art is said to have occurred in the 19th century. The English painters, J. M. W.

Turner (1775–1851) and John Constable (1776 –1837), were central figures in this discovery. They focused attention on nature itself, which had never been the subject of painting before, and elevated it to the position of paintings' primary subject matter.

However, the natural world that was depicted by these painters remained vague and indistinct. The approach of both Turner and Constable was grounded in the contrast between built objects with clear forms, such as bridges and buildings, and formless, ambiguous natural phenomena. Underlying this contrast was a sort of anthropocentric world view, in which nature is an obscure, unknowable entity beyond human control, that even landscape painters could not transcend.

In Hiroshige's *Sudden Shower...* both the bridge and the rain are rendered in the same geometric, abstract straight lines, and there is neither a contrast between humankind and nature, nor an anthropocentric hierarchy in which human-made objects are superior and nature is inferior. The categories of artificial and natural do not exist in the first place, and all things are placed and layered on the same plane as equivalent and equal entities.

There have been many studies of the differences between Eastern and Western views of nature. One study even found that the brains of Westerners perceive the noises of insects as unpleasant intrusions, while those of Japanese process both music and insect noises in the same area of the brain. It is not the goal of this text to probe deeply into such matters, but the way in which the lines of *Sudden Shower...* place the human-made and the natural on the same plane provided significant inspiration for the design of the Hiroshige Museum of Art.

AN ARCHITECTURAL SUDDEN SHOWER

I felt that the design of the Hiroshige Museum of Art, which stores and exhibits Hiroshige's works, ought to resemble a 'sudden shower', but the question was how could this be expressed architecturally?

First, a decision was made to use Yamizo cedar, which is a beautiful variety of cedar from the Yamizo Mountains close to the building site. It was the traditional practice of Japanese carpenters to use the finest lumber available in the vicinity of a building, as the trees emerging from the soil and the building would be subject to the same temperature, humidity and sunlight conditions, making the wood less prone to twisting and warping.

The two sets of lines, co-existing within the forested mountains and in the buildings, resonate in the same air, with the same temperature and humidity. As I listened carefully to the resonance of the surrounding environment, a continuous gradation from the stands of cedars in the mountains to the building's exterior and then to the interior appeared in my mind's eye.

Was it possible to produce a gentle gradation from natural environment to built structure and then to the body? Just as Hiroshige's *Sudden Shower*...[53] presents overlapping layers of rain, bridge, river and trees on the opposite riverbank, could layers be used to achieve a continuous flow from the towering cedars in the mountains behind the museum to the small bodies of the human beings occupying the space?

Traditional Japanese buildings are a succession of loose layers, rather than rigid enclosures. In traditional buildings,

a series of transparent or translucent fixtures consisting of lines – glass doors, bamboo blinds, *shoji* screens – form layers that gradually mediate between the natural surroundings and the body inside. The body is also carefully protected by layers of clothing that intervene between it and the natural world, with the *junihitoe* ('twelve-layered') kimono being the ultimate in layered dress.

With the museum, lines consisting of sawn cedar were placed closest to the mountains, the natural environment behind the building. The stand of cedars itself is actually the first set of lines, and sawing it produces lines that are progressively finer and more orderly.

In Hiroshige's work, the rain – in actuality nothing more than an aggregation of water droplets – is abstracted into straight lines, which give the picture a sense of transparency. Here, the same operation was applied to cedar wood. The cross-sectional dimension of the timber was 3 cm × 6 cm (1 ⅕ × 2 ⅖ in.), which gave the lines sharpness and contrasted the thinness of the lines viewed head-on with the depth of those shadows between them. The pitch of the wood was set at 12 cm (4 ⁷⁄₁₀ in.), which left sufficient gaps between the lines to emphasize the space's sense of openness.

Inside that first layer is a layer of glass that separates the outside air from the inside air. The glass is installed without a frame, so its presence is almost imperceptible. Further inside the glass, cedar with the same cross-sectional dimensions is arrayed and wrapped in washi paper. Wrapping the wood in thin white washi paper softens the lines slightly and changes their quality.

Hiroshige was extraordinarily sensitive about the quality of line, on which woodblock prints are entirely reliant. In traditional woodblock printing, the printer who transfers the images to paper is a separate artisan to the woodblock carver, and the finished print has a surprisingly different appearance depending on how the printer defines the lines. Capitalizing on the softness of wood as a material, Hiroshige and his printer consistently gave lines a remarkably diverse range of expressions.

Kandinsky learned much from printmaking, and it offers numerous hints on how to deal with point, line and plane. The process of making a print involves the intervention of many others or, to use Bruno Latour's term, 'many actors'. The artisan who does the printing is one of these actors, as are the woodblock, the pigment and the water. It is through the cooperation and resistance of these actors that the artist comes into contact with the secrets of the points, lines and planes behind the forms and colours.

Shono comes from *The 53 Stations of the Tokaido*, another series by Hiroshige, and demonstrates the high degree of attention paid to the quality of line. Very slight differences in the thicknesses of lines express depth, so that three-dimensional space emerges from a flat surface. This approach stands in contrast to that of Western painters, who focused on the shapes and silhouettes they could render using lines. *Shono* depicts neither form nor colour, only layers of lines. We do not know what relation this bears to the actual Shono, one of the 53 Tokaido stations, but we do know that Hiroshige used the subject to experiment with lines, and to explore their relationships with the world.

Within the Hiroshige Museum of Art, beyond the lines covered in washi paper, are *shoji* screens made with the *taiko-bari* ('drum-stretching') papering technique, in which washi paper is stretched over a frame of thin cedar planks. This meant that I now had three layers: the first consisting of bare cedar, the second of cedar wrapped in washi paper and the third of washi covering the surface of a screen, with the cedar receding to let the softness of the washi take centre stage. The dimensions in all three layers remain the same, but the quality of the lines changes depending on how the washi is applied. While the quality of the line changes, the rhythm created by the 12 cm (4 $\frac{7}{10}$ in.) pitch of the lines is unchanged. In this way, the rhythm is the same, but the instrument, or the way it is played, is different in each part.

By modifying the lines in this gradated way and creating layers with different qualities of line, I attempted to smoothly connect the natural surroundings and the body, the outside and the inside. In Asia, which traditionally did not utilize perspective rendering, this approach has been refined over many centuries, to a level that astonished Van Gogh and Wright.

THE LINE-DRAWING METHOD
AND THE V&A DUNDEE

While designing the Hiroshige Museum of Art, I was confronted with a question: what is the difference between natural and artificial lines?

The museum design's basic principle was a gradation from the rough, raw, natural lines of stands of cedars in the mountains behind to the innermost layer consisting of thin, abstract lines manifested as shadows behind washi paper. The cedar trees on the mountain slopes still had their bark, and were randomly arranged. Hiroshige was deeply versed in the meaning and effect of random lines, and when depicting rain, he interspersed these random lines into the simple rhythm generated by thin, uniform lines, as seen in *Shono*. He understood that the essence of nature lies in its variability, and expressed this by incorporating lines at various angles into the steady parallel stream of rain. Lines rendered by a man were thus transformed into forces of nature.

For the design of the V&A Dundee (2018)[54] design museum in Scotland, we applied a similar method to the exterior walls. Dundee is located on the River Tay, and the V&A building site is on the southern edge of the city, facing the mouth of the river. We designed the building to extend out over the river, and part of the building is actually constructed in the water. This differs from the way in which buildings are usually constructed; most often they are built at a distance from nature and belong to a different realm, to protect them from natural threats.

54 V&A Dundee (2018). Scotland.

Emphasizing the differences and distance between nature and built structures has been a fundamental principle of Western architectural design, and to highlight the differences, structures are elevated on plinths and held aloft on slender columns (pilotis). Modernist architecture of the 20th century embraced the piloti, and was the legitimate heir to this traditional Western approach.

By contrast, we hoped to create something that would seamlessly join nature (the river) and the city by constructing right in the river. But what would be an appropriate form for an intermediate object between the natural and the human-made?

Inspiration came from the coastal cliffs of the Orkney Islands, off the north coast of Scotland. At the interface between land and water, there can be no pure geometry. The land and water contain so much intrinsic chaos that the cliffs where they meet are inevitably twisted, disparate and riotous. Cliffs rising from the sea are the manifestation of an eternal struggle between sea and land, deviating from simple geometry and entering the realm of folds (aggregations of random lines). Like Hiroshige's rain, the roaming, complex lines encompass an infinite amount of noise.

Our goal was to build a structure as rough as those cliffs at the boundary between sea and land. To build these 'cliffs' with human hands, we used precast concrete in the form of long rods – not concrete cast in place at the site, but concrete components manufactured in a factory. Shadows emerged in the spaces between the lines of precast concrete, and the idea was to use these to produce the richly shadowed texture of a cliff. In other words, we sought to deploy precast concrete lines and harness the power of shadows between them to approach a natural cliff, and to draw close to the complex, ever-changing essence of nature using a line-drawing method rather than a pointillist approach. The shadows in the spaces varied according to the change of season, revealing different expressions: the lines were there to create the spaces, and it was the spaces that played the leading role.

We conducted a variety of computer-based studies on the length, angle and installation of the lines. What sort of noise or randomness could be applied to precast concrete – a linear industrial product – to achieve a degree of coarseness close to that of nature?

To begin with, there were a near-infinite number of potential sizes for the precast rods, as well as their cross-section, shape and surface texture. This meant there were innumerable combinations of small units to explore, and the only way to select the right one for this unique site on the Dundee waterfront was to carry out calculations and trial-and-error experiments using digital technology.

Our firm has been endeavouring to collect countless small dots and lines, and to draw closer to nature, not only with the V&A Dundee, but also with various other projects. This is the basis of our current pointillist and line-drawing approaches. Just as Georges Seurat abandoned solid colour planes and turned to myriad small dots in his attempts to capture the living sea in oil paint, we too harness the potential of countless dots and lines to draw as close as possible to nature. Digital technology aids us in this quest, and for V&A Dundee we were eventually able to extract the noise, randomness and ambiguity we sought from the endless options served up by the computer.

In the middle of the random aggregation of precast concrete is a large hole, or rather 'cave', in the side of the 'cliff'. The cave faces straight towards Union Street, the main street of Dundee, and the goal is for the city's residents to be attracted by the gaping cavern and drawn to the cliff-like structure on the bank of the river.

As with many waterside cities, the waterfront in Dundee used to be a run-down area lined with warehouses that lacked signs of human life. It was the kind of human-made ruin that industrialized societies have produced all over the world. However, with insights from Hiroshige, the creation of a 'cliff' that appears to be somewhere between natural and artificial has reconnected the city to the river and to nature.

LIVING LINES AND DEAD LINES

In thinking about the liberation of lines, I derived many insights from *Lines: A Brief History* (2007), by the British social anthropologist Tim Ingold (b. 1948). Ingold divides lines into two categories, which he calls 'threads' and 'traces', although his original concern was not with lines, but with the distinction between speech and song.

In ancient times in the West, music was interpreted as a linguistic art: words and sounds were conflated, and the essence of music was thought to be synonymous with the resonances of words. At some point, however, music came to be recognized as wordless song with no linguistic element. Music lost its words, and language became silent.

As Ingold considered how this happened, he came to the conclusion that the action of writing may have given rise to this silence. Similarly, I began thinking of lines as belonging to two categories: the free, all-embracing thread, and the trace that is the result of imprinting and describing the movement of thread in a flat, two-dimensional space.

Ingold's categorization of lines recalls the two definitions of lines in quantum mechanics described in this book's introduction: for a tiny ant, a hose is a space over which it can move freely both vertically and horizontally, but for a large bird, the hose is a constrained space allowing movement in only one direction. Modern quantum mechanics has thus redefined lines – and dimensions themselves – in relative terms.

However, Ingold's classification of lines into threads and traces differs slightly to that of quantum mechanics,

as Ingold also introduces the concept of time. In this way, lines are either 'living' lines that are free and continuously generated, or 'dead' lines left behind after the fact, as traces of generation.[55] This contrast recalls the difference between core pressing and surface pressing in traditional Japanese wood-frame construction. Pieces of wood defined by core pressing appear to be living lines, while those defined by surface pressing appear to be dead, superficial lines, slain by sawing.

LINES AND THE THEORY OF TOUCH

I sometimes wonder if the life and death of lines is so clear-cut. The calligrapher Kyuyo Ishikawa's theory of touch revolves around the idea that the boundary between living and dead lines is not as clear as Ingold makes it out to be. It is precisely because Ishikawa (b. 1945) is a working calligrapher, in daily conversation with the line through body and brush, that he is able to penetrate and engage directly with this boundary.

Ishikawa points out that hard Western drawing implements (such as pens and pencils) and soft Eastern implements (such as calligraphy brushes) differ in terms of the gesture of drawing a line, and the mark that results from that gesture (*Hisshoku no kozo* [The Anatomy of Brushstroke], 1992). With a hard utensil, the sharp edge cuts into surfaces – even hard ones – giving the artist the feeling of being fully in control. However, with a soft utensil there is interplay between applied force and repulsive force. In other words, Ishikawa concludes, lines written with hard Western-style drawing utensils are dead lines – traces of actions – while soft Eastern-style lines are lines that continue living, unwilling or unable to die due to the nonalignment of subject and object.

Ishikawa also touches on the colours of sumi ink and Western ink. It is difficult to make out any gradation in the black tones of Western ink, which creates dead lines, whereas lines made with Eastern sumi ink have light and dark variations and blurring,[56] so are perceived as alive.

56 Japanese calligraphy. *Poem on Meditation | Poem about Snow* by Hakuin Ekaku. Edo period. 1615–1868.

LINES WANDERING BETWEEN
LIFE AND DEATH

At the Hiroshige Museum of Art, the boundary between the
building and the forest behind it is negated through gradation, from lines of cedar timber to lines wrapped in Japanese
paper. My aim here was to blend the human-made smoothly
into the natural, with living lines and lines in varying states
of death arranged on a continuum.

However, when I was designing the Birch Moss Chapel
(2015) in a birch wood in Karuizawa,[57] I wanted to take this
a step further. In a birch grove, the trees rise out of the earth
as living lines, and the idea was to use these same birch
trees – chopped to a certain length – as columns to support
the roof. The structure of the building would consist of a
group of living lines with their bark still attached, which
would be hidden or nestled amid a grove of birch trees.
This would juxtapose literal living lines (the growing birch

57 Birch Moss Chapel 2015 . Karuizawa. Japan. pillars support the glass roof.

trees) with lines that are not quite dead (the cut birch with bark), showing how vague and uncertain the boundaries are between life and death, nature and artifice, and enabling the structure to wander on the border.

Making columns out of raw birch trunks was a technical challenge, but an assembly of fine steel wires made it possible to support the roof with the trunks. We worked hard to synchronize the rhythm produced by this artificial forest, made of specially created lines, and the natural birch forest that surrounds it; the random rhythm of the living forest needed to segue into the rhythm of the structured birch lines, without a clear boundary between them.

While pondering living and dead birches, I realized something important: a tree, even while living, is actually dying little by little. As it grows year-by-year and accumulates rings, it gradually stores dead matter inside it, and it is by amassing and increasing the volume of dead matter that the tree builds a sturdy body capable of withstanding wind and water and surviving in a harsh natural environment.

In this way, trees live by slowly dying, and they die more than grass does.

Yet even after a tree is cut down, it still seems as if the wood is alive, expanding, contracting and breathing in response to changes in temperature and humidity. After a cypress tree is cut, its fragrance lingers long afterwards, crying out that it is still alive. Like brush-drawn East Asian calligraphy, the lines of wood drift back and forth between life and death.

As important as – or perhaps even more important than – the placement of the columns for the Birch Moss Chapel was continuity with the earth. We took the step of introducing the moss that covers the forest floor onto the floor of the building, effectively extending the birch grove into the chapel's interior. Transparent acrylic benches were placed on top of the moss garden inside the structure to avoid disturbing the continuity of the floor.

We felt it was important that the floor supporting the occupants and the earth itself were continuous, and this lies at the heart of James Gibson's Affordance Theory. Gibson's discovery was that organisms do not measure the depth of space with the stereoscopic vision of their left and right eyes, but with various particles and lines in the horizontal plane of reference that enable them to gauge depth and measure and control space. Because there is a reference plane, the points and lines affiliated with that plane play melodies and generate rhythms together. Without a reference plane, no matter how many points and lines there are, neither rhythm nor music is generated, and the organism cannot live in an environment and make it its own.

Gibson's Affordances beautifully explain the significance of lines incised in the floors of traditional Japanese buildings – for example, the edges of tatami mats, or the joints between slats applied to surfaces. Another example is the floorboards of stages used in traditional Japanese Noh theatres, which have a fixed width of 18 *shaku* (5.5 m or 17.9 feet). As most of the performer's view is blocked by the mask worn, the Noh actor can feel the lines on the floor with the soles of their feet, count the lines and gauge their position before taking each step.

Tatami mats have standard dimensions not only to make it easy to take them with you when you move, or to measure the area of a room. They also let you quickly gauge the depth of a space, to measure the distance between an object and yourself in an instant, and to confirm one's own location. The lines of tatami make the space one's own. The edges of mats are emphasized by lines of patterned fabric, and if you look closer, other bundles of lines consisting of the fibres of rushes appear, indicating your location and enabling you to gauge your walking speed with a higher degree of accuracy.

THE LINES OF ULTRAFINE CARBON FIBRES

To date, our thinnest and most delicate lines were achieved with Komatsu Seiren Fabric Laboratory Fa-Bo, on a site facing the Sea of Japan in Nomi City, Ishikawa Prefecture. It began when we were called on to strengthen an old three-storey concrete office building's seismic resistance. This is something that is usually carried out by adding steel pipes or H-beams, as these types of steel rod – strong lines produced by industry – are considered the most suitable material for improving a building's resistance to earthquakes.

However, there is something quite wretched looking about a building reinforced with steel braces – they look like

58 Komatsu Seiren Fabric Laboratory Fa-Bo 2015. Nomi. Japan.
Earthquake reinforcement with carbon fibre.

the restless ghosts of lines generated by the industrialized society of the 20th century. I had long wondered if it was possible to reinforce buildings against earthquakes using finer, more delicate lines, and as it was a textile company whose concrete building we were reinforcing, we proposed using carbon fibres, which are analogous to textiles.

It was a challenge to achieve flexible seismic reinforcement using thin carbon fibre wires, but unlike steel, carbon fibre has the advantage that it does not rust when exposed to sea winds. Carbon fibre also has 10 times the tensile strength of steel wire, yet is surprisingly lightweight and does not stretch due to heat. The fact that it does not expand or contract with changes to the thermal conditions means that it does not need to be re-tightened periodically, and its performance as a wire is outstanding.

Steel beams were embedded in the ground around the building, and these were connected to the building with the 'magic threads' of carbon fibre.[58] The exterior walls and interior partition walls also needed to be reinforced, so we used thin strands of carbon fibre there as well.

In contrast to the rough look of steel that is typically used to reinforce a structure, the carbon fibre lines were a gentle and delicate addition to the blocky concrete building. Next to its thick frame of concrete columns and beams the carbon fibres look like spider webs and, like the threads of a web, are not only fine, but also soft, supple and tenacious. The spider web threads describe curved surfaces, while connecting the earth and the building, and these curved surfaces waver between sky and ground on the Sea of Japan coast like the Northern Lights. If we could design a structure with such organic lines, we might be able to revive the living lines that Gaudí and Art Nouveau pursued, only to end in frustration.

SILK-LIKE LINES OF THE TOMIOKA WAREHOUSE

Clad in thin carbon fibre wire, Fa-Bo can be seen as a resurgent underdog, following half a century of failure of the new architecture of lines that Kenzō Tange was unable to achieve. Tange wanted to go beyond the linear H-beam and I-beam architecture of the 20th century, which was perfected by Mies and became the uniform of the industrialized society led by the US, the culture of concrete and steel. Indeed, the two materials go hand in hand: concrete would not be able to bear load or withstand earthquakes without the reinforcing steel bars inside it. Concrete is a mass of points – gravel, sand, limestone – bound together by the lines of steel. In this sense both concrete construction and the auto industry – engines of the 20th century – were propelled by the hard lines of steel.

This modern era in architecture began when Filippo Brunelleschi, the son of a goldsmith, learned the lessons of line from metal and used it to realize his great dome in Florence. The history of modern architecture, from Brunelleschi's lines to Mies van der Rohe's steel-framed skyscrapers, is the history of line itself, with metal playing a leading role. The modern state and steel have been inseparably linked.

But is there a kind of line that can replace metal? When I encountered carbon fibre, I was struck by the idea that it is time we graduated from metal lines. If we could do this, we might be able to bring about a major turning point in post-Renaissance architecture, which has relied on metal in terms of both design and structure.

At Fa-Bo, carbon fibre was used to reinforce a concrete building, but with the Tomioka Warehouse – another seismic retrofitting project – even more delicate carbon fibre was used to reinforce a wooden building.[59] The Tomioka Warehouse was built to store silk in Tomioka, a city famed for its silk and textiles, so seismic reinforcement with thread seemed like the optimal solution for Tomioka.

The seismic retrofitting of wooden structures is more difficult than one might think. The most common method used is to insert diagonal members known as braces, but these bulky wooden braces can easily ruin the charm of wooden buildings.

Slender steel braces are another option, but because steel is a heavier material than wood, it makes the building as a whole heavier, and to compensate for that weight, even bulkier steel braces are needed. The delicacy of wood-frame construction is completely lost in this vicious cycle.

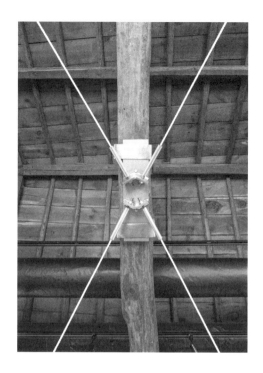

59 Tomioka Warehouse 2018 . Japan.
By applying carbon fibre. we reinforced
the wooden warehouse. built 100 years
ago to withstand big earthquakes.

The beauty of wood-frame architecture lies in its use of a
lightweight material to create remarkably sturdy structures
capable of withstanding powerful earthquakes. When bulky
wooden braces or hefty steel are introduced, this peaceful,
orderly, lightweight world is shattered, but with a strong
and light material like carbon fibre, wooden structures
can both retain their lightness and at the same time gain
seismic resistance.

We worked with a structural engineer, Yasuhiko Ejiri,
on the Tomioka Warehouse project, looking for the most
efficient way to reinforce the wooden structure. Ejiri has a
track record of reinforcing important cultural properties
with carbon fibre, including Kiyomizu-dera Temple in
Kyoto and Zenko-ji Temple in Nagano. When reinforcing
sites of such historic importance, it is crucial that the

reinforcing materials are not visible, so carbon fibre is installed in places where it cannot be seen, such as attics.

At the Tomioka Warehouse we intentionally had the white lines of carbon fibre running through the air. A cat's-cradle formation like this cannot be made with steel or stainless steel wire, as it will break at the points of contact where wires bend around one another. Unless additional hardware is inserted at the contact points, the wires will not be interconnected and the structure will fail. However, since carbon fibre is a kind of thread, a cat's-cradle formation can be made without any weakness at the contact points, and be realized directly in a practical structure.

Unlike the 'dead' lines of steel, which require additional joints to be inserted at their intersections, and are thus constrained by those contact points, the lines of a cat's cradle are free and living – the value of which Ingold noted in *Lines: A Brief History*. They are not static traces of action, but dynamic threads that run through the air with the suppleness of dancers, alive and in pursuit of a new system of geometry. We produced a cat's cradle at Tomioka Warehouse, dreaming of the day when architecture outgrows metal and we can create structures with living threads. In the city of silk we endeavoured to turn a new page in the history of the line.

PLANE

RIETVELD VS DE KLERK

With its remarkable rigidity, viscosity and airtightness, concrete was the material of choice for producing the massive volumes needed to accommodate the exploding population and economy of the 20th century. However, these volumes felt oppressive and uncomfortable, and attempts were made to dismantle them and create airy, light spaces.

The De Stijl (Dutch for 'The Style') group was formed by a collection of young architects in the Netherlands who endeavoured to deconstruct volumes using thin planes. One of the leading figures in De Stijl was Gerrit Rietveld (1888–1964), who had a major impact on the architectural world with his thorough disassembly of volumes in Rietveld Schröder House (1924).[60]

Like his father, Rietveld began his career as a furniture maker, so it was perhaps easier for him to realize an architecture of planes – after all, the volumes of architecture need to be closed, but those of furniture do not. However, in Europe, with its harsh winter climate, enclosure is a fundamental prerequisite for buildings. The same is not true in milder Japan, and in *Essays in Idleness*, the medieval essayist Yoshida Kenkō noted that 'a house should be built with the summer in mind'.

In the conservative context of European architecture, Rietveld derived a compositional approach that employed thin planes. In furniture, planes and other planes, or planes and lines, can be combined to form pieces without producing closed structures; anything that uses lines and planes

60 Rietveld Schroder House. Utrecht. Netherlands.

to support or enfold a body or an object can be a piece of furniture. Rietveld thought it would be desirable for architecture to have a similar kind of loose, free-form relationship with the body, and arrived at the Rietveld Schröder House, a 'house-sized piece of furniture'.

Rietveld is equally well known for his constructivist chairs, but what interests me more than these are the wooden chairs designed by Michel de Klerk (1884–1923). De Klerk was a Dutch architect of the generation preceding Rietveld's, and with his pupil, Pieter Kramer (1881–1961), he sought to marry the rustic simplicity of Dutch thatched farmhouses to modern lifestyles, by incorporating straw twine and armrests with soft lines that fit snugly to the body.

In Japan, the modernist design pioneer Sutemi Horiguchi (1895–1984), who co-founded Bunri-ha (the Secessionist School), was greatly influenced by the designs of De Klerk and his pupils. Horiguchi combined thatching and boxy modern structures in his Shien-so house (1926), which stunned the pre-war Japanese architecture scene and heralded the emergence of a young genius.

Both De Klerk and Horiguchi conceived modernism as a critique of mainstream trends of the day, in particular industrialization. In both the Netherlands and Japan, thatched roofs were a basic element of farmhouse design at the time and both of these designers believed that the task of the 20th century – and of modernism – was to restore this type of naturalness and simplicity.

Modernist architecture, however, went on to thoroughly embrace industrialization, and quickly moved towards mass-produced structures made of concrete and steel. Following World War II, the flexible planes and lines advocated by De Klerk and Horiguchi were forgotten completely, and the next generation – which included Le Corbusier and Kenzō Tange – rejected Horiguchi as an outmoded humanist. His career stymied, Horiguchi immersed himself in the study of tea rooms at Jiko-in Temple in Nara, where his achievements as a researcher were significant.

Looking at the farmhouse-inspired furniture designed by De Klerk reveals a human, physical logic that cannot be contained in the rationalist framework of mass-production and industrialization. The elbow rests of De Klerk's chairs consist of woven straw ropes that hang slackly, aesthetically unrelated to the geometric elegance of the overall piece. However, once the sitter's arms are rested on the ropes, the ropes gently support the body, and the living lines (ropes) and the living object (body) strike up a lively conversation. The voices emanating from De Klerk's furniture cannot be heard in the rigid planes of Rietveld.

RIETVELD VS MIES

The Rietveld Schröder House is by far the 'lightest' early 20th-century Modernist building. When asked to name masterpieces of early modernism, one would normally cite Le Corbusier's Villa Savoye (1931) and Mies van der Rohe's Barcelona Pavilion (1929), but when architecture is reassessed in terms of points, lines and planes, the Rietveld Schröder House's lightness of touch surpasses that of the other two.

Villa Savoye is a perfect example of architecture of floating volume, which simply takes a standard 20th-century volume and elevates it from the ground. The mere act of causing it to float created the illusion that it was something unique, which perhaps shows the genius of Le Corbusier. However, the levitating volume actually becomes more impoverished as a space as the building's connection with the earth is diminished, and the aerial garden that was one of Le Corbusier's selling points is underwhelming. It is perhaps unsurprising that the Villa Savoye clients sued Le Corbusier.

Meanwhile, the detailing of the columns in the Barcelona Pavilion clearly shows that Mies was not only interested in, but also obsessed with the deconstruction of volumes. To the average viewer, columns come across as lines, but to Mies, columns were dull, weighty volumes. Naturally, columns need to be thick in order to bear the weight of a building and withstand earthquakes, but this was something Mies could not bear. So, instead of making steel columns with square pipes, he employed sharp-edged, cross-shaped

61 An interior view of Barcelona Pavilion. Catalonia. Spain.

planar elements, reducing the volume of the columns and stimulating the eye with keen lines. In this way, Mies succeeded in turning steel columns that could easily become volumes, into slim lines.

The walls of the Barcelona Pavilion are also quite thin.[61] To achieve this, the bricks supporting the stone were first laid in a non-standard direction, so as to create a slender wall. When thin stone was applied on top of this wall, it resulted in a total wall thickness of only 17 cm (6 $^7/_{10}$ in.). This is almost half the standard dimension (30 cm / 11 $^4/_5$ in.) of overlaying stone on both sides of a concrete wall — a common practice of the time. As the son of a stonemason, Mies was well versed in the use of the material, and his thin stone walls give the space a taut, tense feeling, although even that could not match the furniture-like thinness of the Rietveld Schröder House.

However, to me, the thin planes of the Rietveld Schröder House still look too thick and hard, and the house's Constructivist manipulation of form, which aims to make the whole look lightweight with its clever assembly (composition) of planes and lines, has what strikes me as an overly deliberate intellectualism and anthropocentrism.

Constructivism can be described as a desperate measure to conceal the bulky volumetric quality of 20th-century design. Points, lines and planes move about freely and lightly, but the freer the composition, the more prominent the arbitrary decisions of the all-powerful designer become, and therefore the more intellectual and distasteful it runs the risk of becoming. Constructivism actually exacerbates the ponderous and outmoded quality of the compositional elements, and this tediousness comes across in Kandinsky's detailed description of the Constructivist approach in *Point and Line to Plane*.

DISCOVERING BEDOUIN FABRICS IN THE SAHARA

In *Lines: A Brief History* (2007), Tim Ingold characterizes two types of lines: traces and threads. Similarly, I feel there are two kinds of planes, which I describe as trajectories (dead planes as traces of something) and threads (networks of threads forming living planes that move freely like textiles in space).

Rietveld's planes, while thin, seem to me to belong to the dead category. By contrast, the living planes I seek are – to use a metaphor from superstring theory in quantum mechanics – planes that continuously oscillate between their dual natures as particles and waves, with the freedom of strings.

Simply making planes thinner does not make them as supple as fabric, but is it possible to produce thin and supple

62 Bedouin tent beneath Erg Chebbi sand dunes in the Sahara Desert near Merzouga. Morocco.

planes that move in accordance with flow and change? If a flexible object is subjected to force or action, it will surely move in response, and if such flexible planes could be introduced into architecture, they could be useful tools for dismantling heavy volumes.

As I was thinking along these lines, I recalled the Bedouin tents I had seen on a research trip to the Sahara Desert in graduate school. They were simple tents consisting of thin tree-branch poles stuck into the sand, with fabric stretched over them.[62] A nomadic people, the Bedouin traverse the Sahara with these branches and pieces of fabric on their camels' backs. The thin membranes of their tents can withstand the harsh Saharan climate, and underpin their nomadic lifestyle.

Our six-member village survey team, led by Professor Hiroshi Hara, was also a tent-dwelling tribe: we followed the Bedouin's example and slept in small tents, with thin plastic poles and nylon fabric, as we travelled through the Sahara Desert. However, while our Japanese-made tents were compact, foldable and excellent in terms of mobility, when we were invited into a Bedouin tent and served tea, I felt our tents could never compare to the beauty and comfort of their fabrics.

I could tell that these fabrics were an essential part of Bedouin culture. Fabric is laid and folded in layers over the sand, forming a floor that defines the relationship between their bodies and the desert. While the temperature drops drastically on winter nights in the desert, the Bedouin respond by layering fabric between their body and the sand, creating a soft cocoon-like area that enfolds their body. In this way, single pieces of fabric define the relationship between the earth and their bodies, and thin pieces of fabric reflecting their deft skill define the relationship between them and the sky.

Fabric is integral to the everyday life of the Bedouin. At the time of our trip, the 'boom box' (portable radio and cassette deck) had also evidently become a necessity for the desert dwellers, and they carried them on their shoulders in specially designed fabric bags. These bags were so beautiful that they could make a cheap plastic boom box look like something else entirely, demonstrating how fabric planes have the power to alter lifestyles and transform the world.

SEMPER VS. LAUGIER

Gottfried Semper (1803–1879) was the most prominent architectural theorist of the 19th century. He developed his own unique view of architecture, which was rooted in an extraordinary degree of interest in fabrics in planar form – textiles – and in the process of weaving.

The idea that a building begins with a frame dominated the thinking of European architects from the Renaissance onwards. Frame-based theory is line-based theory, in that a frame is a sturdy assembly of lines. The frame-oriented theory is exemplified by Marc-Antoine Laugier's *An Essay on Architecture* (1753), which states that architecture began with a framework of wooden poles. Laugier's allegorical drawing[63] appears in many architectural textbooks, illustrating the dawn of architecture, and rigid frames remain the prevailing type of building structure today. Whenever I see a rigid post-and-beam structure being erected on a construction site, I am confronted with the fact that Laugier's frame theory remains the basis of architecture and dominates the human-made environment.

By contrast, although traditional Japanese wooden buildings are often thought of as rigid-frame structures because they are assemblies of columns and beams, they are not rigid frames. In fact, they are not frames at all. Unlike a rigid frame, the points of contact between the columns and beams are not firmly fastened, but simply engaged and linked without bolts or nails. In terms that Semper might have used, the columns and beams are no more than braided together.

63 Marc-Antoine Laugier,
frontispiece for *Essai Sur
l'Architecture*, 1755 edition.

But how could such loose-jointed structures survive in
an earthquake-prone country like Japan? The secret is that
the columns and beams are connected by various flexible
mechanisms, including sections of wall, transoms, sliding
doors and *shoji* screens. Unlike stone or brick masonry,
Japanese earthen walls were also soft, and their connec-
tions to columns and beams were weak and easily split in
the event of an earthquake. However, this unreliability
actually allowed them to absorb the force of earthquakes
and Japanese wooden buildings have withstood earthquakes thanks to a pliable system that absorbs seismic
forces through elements such as sliding doors and *shoji*
screens (which look even more unreliable than the walls
in an earthquake).

Through experience, the Japanese came to the conclusion that the less rigid a structure was, the more earthquake-resistant it would actually be as a result, and these pliable 'intercolumnar' mechanisms have also been utilized elsewhere in the world. In Europe, the Rhine River valley is known for major fault lines and earthquakes, and wooden columns and beams with sections of wall in their interstices have become the norm. Through their repeated experiences with earthquakes, the people living in the region arrived at the same conclusion as that of Japanese wooden structures.

Semper also rejected Laugier's frame theory and defined architecture as covering rather than frame. Semper believed that coverings could exist without frames, and as such he was a pioneer in 'thinking outside the frame'. It is believed that his inspiration came from a frontier village exhibited at the World's Fair, the premier international event of the 19th century.

Semper was designing the layout for the Great Exhibition (as the 1851 London World's Fair at Crystal Palace was known) and was profoundly impressed by the primitive dwellings he saw there. Just as I was impressed by the fabric abodes of the Bedouin, Semper's encounter with remote settlements from outside Europe made him realize the importance of fabrics and gave rise to his textile model of architecture. The fact that Semper's father was in the textile business may have been related, although the fabrics his father dealt in would not have been as free form and flexible as those of remote regions.

A FABRIC TEA ROOM IN FRANKFURT

I came into contact with Bedouin tents just before my architectural career began, and thereafter I secretly hoped to someday produce architecture of fabrics and thin, flexible planes like that of the Bedouin. However, opportunities to design structures with fabrics rarely came my way. My first opportunity came at the Frankfurt Museum of Applied Arts, in Semper's home country of Germany, where I was able to realize a fabric structure for the first time in a garden beside the Rhine River (2007).

Mr. Schneider, the museum's director at the time, told me as soon as we met that he wanted me to build a tea room in the museum garden. 'But,' he said, 'not with wood and earthen walls, as you usually would. We have vandals in Germany who will tear it to pieces overnight.'

So, was I supposed to design a tea room with concrete or heavy steel plates? Was he asking me to reject my own principles, which I had adhered to so far, of 'architecture of defeat' and 'weak architecture'? At a loss, I decided to calm down, regroup and formulate a strategy back in Japan.

Returning to Japan and cooling my head a bit, I had what I thought was a pretty bright idea: to construct an instant tea room that could be easily assembled from fabric, then folded into a small package and stored in the museum's storehouse after use. It was an idea, born out of a certain desperation, which took the client's proposal and turned it on its head.

When I feel I am under attack, my approach is not to grapple face to face, but to fight back indirectly, using the other party's logic against them. When doing this it is crucial to have the solid technical grounds for an idea, even if it is an outlandish one that has little chance of being approved. The details must be worked out in terms of feasible possibilities, not dreams and visions, and a high-quality model is also crucial. If you can demonstrate seriousness in this way, the other party may be convinced, but there is never a 100 per cent guarantee. In this instance, though, Director Schneider gave the go-ahead for an instant fabric tea room at our next meeting, so neither the model nor the design drawings went to waste.

An instant fabric tea room could be created in a variety of ways: it could be a tent with wooden poles like those of the Bedouin, or a tent like those we used in the Sahara, consisting of a light framework with fabric stretched over it. However, if someone tried to design this kind of structure and have it meet contemporary standards for seismic-resistance, the frame – even of a fabric building – would be necessarily bulky, and become the main feature of the building. This deviated from my intent, which was to reject Laugier's frame-oriented approach and move towards Semper's style of textile-like architecture.

Seeking an instant structure in which fabric could play the leading role, I came up with the idea of injecting air between two layers of membrane. I wanted to show the process of turning on the compressor and allowing the double membrane to expand with the force of air to create the tea room. The swelling sheets of fabric were living planes, so I was pursuing living lines (threads) and planes (textiles) that were being generated continuously, rather than dead lines and planes (trajectories) as traces.

An added advantage was that the air between the two layers of membrane served as thermal insulation, making it possible to design a tea room that would be comfortable even in Frankfurt's cold winters. Semper's textile-oriented architecture is rooted in the principle of gathering materials suited to the environment and climate of the site, interweaving them and creating a covering that results in a comfortable environment. It is not based on Laugier's rigid principle that a frame must first be in place, but on a principle of adaptation: if it is cold, add layers of fabric.

As mentioned previously, modern computer technology has restored additive processes to architecture. The additive quality of pre-Renaissance architecture faded after Leon Battista Alberti, and the world came to be dominated by impoverished architecture based on subtraction. Concrete is highly compatible with subtraction, while fabric, which can be layered, is the material most geared towards addition.

The most difficult aspect of the Frankfurt project was finding a fabric that would not wear out, even after being inflated hundreds or thousands of times. Dome stadiums are a type of membranous structure, but the membranes used for those are not designed to be disassembled, transported and erected again in a nomadic way – once up, they remain in place. These domes also look like they are made of concrete, so hard and oppressively heavy that it is impossible to relax and enjoy watching sports. As for the white PVC used for schools' field-day tents and so forth, it is not durable enough to be repeatedly folded and unfolded. It is almost as if our lifestyles have become so static and rigid that we have lost the fungible fabrics of nomadic life.

The fabric we eventually found was Tenara, developed and manufactured by W. L. Gore & Associates. With a thickness of only 0.38 mm ($\frac{1}{100}$ in.), it is far thinner than the membrane of a domed stadium, and possesses outstanding

64 Tee Haus (2007), Frankfurt. Germany. Temporary tea room built as a double-membrane structure.

flexibility and permeability. The fabric allows plenty of sunlight through, even when it is double-layered, and when threads are stretched at a pitch of about 60 cm (23 ³⁄₅ in.) between two membranes, the desired shape can be achieved when air is introduced.[64] As the lines of threads can be seen from the interior, this is not only an example of an architecture of planes, but it also has the delicacy of an architecture of threads (lines).

The overall shape of the tea room is like that of a peanut, with two convex bulges intersecting in the centre. One bulge is the guest space, where tea is served, and the other is the kitchen where the tea is prepared. A folding screen stands between the two, gently dividing them while the whole remains connected.

Unlike the Rietveld Schröder House or the Barcelona Pavilion, which consist of rigid planes, structures consisting of supple planes allow the soft and subtle alteration and manipulation of space. Space can be squeezed, twisted and distorted at will. Even something as ambiguous and understated as simultaneously connecting and separating tea-drinking and tea-preparation areas is easy to achieve using fabric. When planes are alive in this way, various situations and actions can be juxtaposed and layered within them; as in a Bedouin tent, various actions and aspects of life overlap.

FRANK LLOYD WRIGHT'S DESERT ENCAMPMENT

After we completed this membranous structure on the banks of the Rhine in Frankfurt, another membrane project came along, this time in the wilds of Hokkaido. A friend of mine had acquired a plot of land in the town of Taiki, near Obihiro, and wanted to build a village of experimental ecological houses there. I took on the task of designing an experimental house that could withstand the harsh climate of Hokkaido and yet be environmentally friendly.

Environmentally friendly or sustainable housing is an urgent issue in modern architecture, and high-performance insulation and solar panels on rooftops have become the standard solutions for sustainability. Of course, those are viable solutions, but the thicker the insulation and the more panels there are on the roof, the heftier and more heavily armoured a building becomes, with results that feel increasingly grandiose. This kind of house would not enable its inhabitants to experience life in the unspoiled wilderness of Hokkaido, and I refused to accept that this was the future of housing.

My intuition said that consideration for the environment did not have to result in such overblown structures, and as

65 Frank Lloyd Wright's Taliesin West. Arizona. USA.

I was contemplating the challenge, two houses provided
me with suggestions. The first was a tent-like house that
Frank Lloyd Wright built at the age of 70. Wright had lung
ailments, and was advised by his doctor to move to a warmer
location to avoid getting pneumonia. Always fond of going
to extremes, Wright decided to move to the desert near
Phoenix, Arizona, and set out to live in a tent-like house on
land where only cactus grew.

Until then, Wright had been based in the town of Spring
Green, Wisconsin, northwest of Chicago and close to his
birthplace. There, he had built a studio and house of brick
and wood,[65] which he named Taliesin after a bard in Celtic
mythology whose name translates as 'shining brow'. The
name reflected Wright's veneration of hard work, which
brings sweat to the brow, and his vision of a shining house
on a hill, where he lived and worked amid lush greenery.

However, at an advanced age, Wright established a new
base of operations in the Arizona desert. He decided to

spend summers in Wisconsin, where it stays relatively cool, and winters in Arizona where it remains warm. He named the Arizona location Taliesin West.

Wright thought his desert home and studio ought to be like an encampment, with structures that were connected to the land and lightweight in the manner of tents. However, using fabric to build a habitable structure in the desert was no easy task, especially for a man of his age. Wright worked with plastic (as well as cotton canvas) to achieve the lightness and flexibility of a tent, but while it is difficult enough to live in the desert, it is even harder in a membranous dwelling. Why did he insist so strongly on the encampment model and fabric-like materials? Many of Wright's staff, who had been instructed to live in the Arizona desert with him, asked that very question. Many responded by leaving.

Today, however, I think I understand Wright's feelings. It is precisely because one lives in a harsh natural environment that one wants to be in touch with nature via a light, tent-like structure. This applies equally to Hokkaido, as it does to the Arizona desert.

FABRIC HOUSE IN TAIKI

Further inspiration for the experimental ecological house came from a dwelling known as a *cise*, which was inhabited by the indigenous Ainu people of Hokkaido. A *cise* is made of *kumazasa* bamboo, which grows wild in the Hokkaido wilderness, and the roof and walls are completely covered with bamboo leaves, making the house soft and fluffy like a stuffed animal.

The leaves of *kumazasa* bamboo are thin, and do not themselves have thermal insulating properties. However, overlaying multiple leaves creates layers of air that serve as insulation, with the air itself shielding people from the winter cold. I felt that this idea could be applied to the air layer between two sheets of fabric, so it too could serve as insulation. If an electric heater could be installed between the two layers of fabric and the heated air circulated, then it might be possible to live in an uninsulated tent, even in the bitter cold of Hokkaido.

I consulted an environmental engineer, Bunpei Magori, who thought the idea interesting and innovative, and immediately began calculating its feasibility. The goal was to build a house that was sufficiently sustainable and environmentally friendly without thick layers of plastic-based insulation. This lack of insulation would also allow sunlight to shine directly into the house, so one could live in the wilderness united with the rhythm of the rising and setting sun. This sense of oneness with the earth is the essence of fabric-based architecture, which Wright sought in the Arizona desert. This, I felt, was real living.

With a *cise*, the ground itself is the floor, on which people sit and lie directly, whereas in a typical Japanese house the floor is elevated to create ventilation between the floor and ground. However, a *cise* had an *irori* hearth at the centre of its earthen-floored space and the Ainu kept a fire burning in the hearth all year round. This would keep the ground constantly warm, and the residual heat of summer lingered even during the harsh winters. By using the ground as a heat storage device, the pliable dwellings of the Ainu were slowly and continuously heated from below.

Regulating the environment of a living space without using active heating and cooling equipment, as in the *cise*, is called passive heating and cooling, and houses constructed in this way are sometimes called 'passive houses'. The *cise*

66 Memu Meadows 2007 . Taiki. Japan. Experimental house designed for cold regions. built in a wooden frame and wrapped by a double membrane.

was a true pioneer of the passive house, and demonstrated how a light and delicate house could be adequately comfortable with the help of the solid ground beneath it.

Following the example of the *cise*, our fabric house – Mêmu Meadows[66] – has a hearth in the middle of the floor, which is directly connected to the earth, and the two breathe in resonance with one another. *Mêmu* means 'spring' (as in water bubbling up from underground) in the Ainu language, and there have been numerous springs in the area since time immemorial.

An interesting thing about fabric houses is that they are also earth-houses. Fabric may appear unreliable at first glance, but precisely because they are soft and delicate, these houses are able to take advantage of the earth's physiology as a living organism. As a result, the fabric house is protected by the land, and as I designed this experimental house, the feeling of sleeping soundly on the warm sand of the Sahara came flooding back to me.

CASA UMBRELLA: SHELTERING PEOPLE IN EMERGENCIES

While concerns about vandalism led to the creation of a fabric tea room in Frankfurt, and the cold climate of Hokkaido helped shape an experimental fabric dwelling in the wilderness, it was catastrophic disasters that underpinned the construction of Casa Umbrella (Umbrella House), a fabric structure in Milan.[67]

The Triennale di Milano is an international design and architecture event held every three years in Milan. In 2007, I received an email from its office with a request for a design proposal for 'Casa per Tutti' (House for Everybody), an exhibition of new types of shelters to shield people from major natural disasters. This was a groundbreaking project for which several architects selected from various countries would design evacuation shelters, to be constructed directly at the Triennale site.

It was a time of successive catastrophes, which had seen the 2004 Indian Ocean earthquake and tsunami, and massive flooding in New Orleans caused by Hurricane Katrina in 2005, with the 2008 Sichuan earthquake in China occurring shortly before the event opened. Although the 2011 Tohoku earthquake and tsunami was a few years off, everyone was starting to feel that the planet was falling apart. With movements of the earth's crust growing more violent and global warming accelerating, there was a visceral sense that any kind of disaster could strike at any time, and I started thinking about how fabric could shield people during times like these.

Fabric has been used for centuries to aid the wounded: bandages have been wrapped around wounds, and compresses used to cool or warm the body. The feel of bed sheets when one is hospitalized is also an unforgettable one. The weaker people get, the more they require the softness and pliability of fabric, with its mysterious healing and soothing powers. This relates to the Bedouin's reliance on fabric in the harsh environment of the Sahara, and Frank Lloyd Wright's desire to use tent-like materials in the Arizona desert.

As I was rereading the title of the exhibition – 'Casa per Tutti' – I was struck by an idea that caused me to break out laughing. *Casa* means 'house' in Italian, but in Japanese, *kasa* means 'umbrella'. Maybe there could be some form of emergency housing that resembled an umbrella? After all, an umbrella uses fabric to protect us from rain or sunlight, so when disaster strikes why not have an umbrella-like housing that could be rapidly erected to shelter people, just as we pop open an umbrella with a swift gesture when it starts to rain?

The first image that came to mind was of a structure that actually resembled a giant umbrella. It would be structurally possible to create such an umbrella by thickening the bones of its 'skeleton', but where would such a huge umbrella be stored? I am aligned with the ideas of Gottfried Semper, who sought to reject the frame and move in the direction of the covering, so I did not want to produce a bulky frame.

My next thought was if the umbrella was the motif, why not take a large number of ordinary umbrellas and connect them to form a single evacuation shelter? Surely most people have an umbrella in their umbrella stand at home, and if an earthquake or tsunami hits it is something they are likely to bring along when evacuating.

67 Casa Umbrella 2008 . Milan. Italy. Temporary house made of 15 umbrellas joined together with zippers.

A story formed in my mind, in which people carrying umbrellas of the same type joined forces, adding their umbrellas to the whole to build a shelter. Connecting or 'weaving' the umbrellas into a structure is in line with Semper's principle of interwoven structures, and resembles the way the caddisfly builds its nest by gathering objects from its surroundings, as discussed previously. It would also fit the theme of 'Casa per Tutti' (House for Everybody): just as small, weak individuals can help one another, so small, weak umbrellas could protect everyone if they are combined to create a larger structure.

FULLER'S DOMES AND THE DEMOCRATIZATION OF ARCHITECTURE

Once a narrative is in place, all that remains is to resolve the technical issues. The brilliant American architect, designer and philosopher, Buckminster Fuller, carried out a series of experiments where small units were assembled to create dome-like structures. Fuller has been a hero of mine since my student days, as he was a pioneer in deconstructing the boxy, rectangular architectural paradigm, and designed a wide range of products, from buildings to cars. He was consistently critical of the elitist, European-style image of the architect, prevalent since the time of Alberti, in which privileged architects designed unique architectural forms for the few, and he kept up a lifelong fight for grassroots, democratized architecture.

Fuller also coined the term 'Spaceship Earth', and was among the first to sound the alarm about the global environment, arguing that using the smallest amount of material to achieve the largest volume in a dome structure was an optimal solution. With his advanced mathematical skills, Fuller proved that regular 12- and 20-sided polygons are suitable for domes, and built numerous geodesic domes (also known as Fuller domes) in workshops with his students. His aim was to demonstrate the feasibility of democratic architecture that anyone can build independently.

Professor Yoshichika Uchida, one of my mentors at university, was also highly enthused about Fuller's ideas. Uchida was critical of Kenzō Tange, his colleague at the

University of Tokyo, and conducted a variety of studies and experiments in an attempt to subvert the paradigm of the architect as an elite formalist in the Tange mode. When Fuller visited Japan as a design consultant for the Yomiuri Shimbun Group, which was planning to build a dome stadium, Professor Uchida served as Fuller's guide and they discussed the future of architecture.

As a student, I tried to design a geodesic dome of my own, but making one was not as easy as Fuller said it would be. It was quite difficult to produce frames for regular 12- and 20-sided polygons, and waterproofing the joints was difficult, which perhaps explains why geodesic domes never became as popular as Fuller had predicted. In the end, they played a limited role as a high-end construction technique for special-purpose buildings, such as the American Pavilion at the 1967 Montreal Expo.[68]

To me, the limitations of geodesic domes stemmed from the way they attempted to solve the problem of dome construction with a Laugier-style frame-oriented approach. Laugier's approach is intellectualist and schematic, and attempts to squeeze a complex and intertwined world into a simplified framework; it wants to force everything to be computable.

A reduction to frames produces the illusion of a solution, but there is a huge gap between frames and reality, and crucial parts of the world spill out like sand from the frame's interstices. If a dome could be built simply by adding small umbrellas one after another, without relying on a frame, then it would come one step closer to Fuller's ultimate ideal of democratic architecture. As someone who aims for a shift from Laugier-derived frame structures to Semper-style woven structures, I wanted to realize a dome for everyone by interconnecting everyday items like umbrellas. In doing

68 The geodesic dome called Biosphere in Montreal. Canada. designed for the Canadian world fair. 1967.

so I could carry on Fuller's struggle and take a step towards the democratization of architecture.

I consulted a structural engineer, Norihiro Ejiri, who instantly understood what I was looking for. He confirmed that it was possible to build a structurally sound dome simply by connecting ordinary umbrellas one to another, without introducing a reinforcing frame.

Apparently, it makes geometric sense to connect 15 umbrellas to form a dome, although using umbrellas as units requires some degree of ingenuity. This is because an umbrella is a hexagonal form consisting of six triangles, but to form a closed dome, each umbrella needs an additional three triangular pieces of fabric to fill the gaps between them. Although this makes the umbrellas' shapes a bit peculiar, the additional fabric has the advantage of making it easier for owners of compatible umbrellas to find one another. The triangular pieces of fabric can also function as windows; while standard geodesic domes are windowless, the umbrella-dome has windows that can be opened and closed with zippers, allowing for ventilation.

Once someone finds five other people with compatible umbrellas, they can connect one umbrella after another using the waterproof zippers attached to the rim of each umbrella. It is the ultimate in Semper-style, caddisfly-like architecture, which allows people to create protective coverings by assembling inexpensive umbrellas. As the skeletons of ordinary umbrellas are much slimmer and lighter than the skeletons of Fuller's geodesic domes, the resulting structure looks like it has no skeleton (frame), only a covering, but how can such a thin skeleton support a dome?

SAVING THE WORLD WITH TENSEGRITY

The structural engineer, Norihiro Ejiri, was confident that the thin skeletons of ordinary umbrellas could support a dome measuring 5.3 metres (17.4 feet) in diameter, as the skeletons and connecting membranes help each other to form a kind of tensegrity structure.

The principal of tensegrity (or tensional integrity) is another extraordinarily efficient structural system exemplifying the genius of Buckminster Fuller, who was always conscious of the finite nature of the planet's resources. On a closed spaceship, if everyone on board did just as they pleased, then everyone would be in big trouble. Fuller felt that with exploding populations and expanding cities, the planet was too small and fragile to act as a spaceship for its ever-growing crew. He drew attention to this by calling our tiny, vulnerable planet 'Spaceship Earth', foretelling exactly the kind of environmental crisis we are facing today.

To make finite resources last longer, Fuller believed that the efficiency of a substance needed to be maximized, and when a substance (steel, for example) is used as a structural material, the highest efficiency is achieved by employing it as a tensile (pulling) member. If a thin steel wire is used as a tensile member, even heavy stone can be lifted, but if steel is used for compressive members (such as columns) or bending members (such as beams), its efficiency is much lower: steel beams need to be thick and bulky in order to support heavy stone.

Fuller discovered that the most efficient structure could be achieved by combining tensile members (wire) and compressive members (rods). He termed this structural system a 'tensegrity structure', as it utilizes tension to attain integrity. If this seemingly magical structural system is used effectively, the resulting building seems to have been constructed in a weightless environment.

I have been interested in tensegrity for a long time, and have experimented with it in various ways. I found the way it enables sturdy structures to be created using thin, thread-like lines to be magical. As each individual compressive member can be seen as a kind of point, a tensegrity structure could be described as a structural system that weaves together points and lines. If one were to pile up points such as stones, the result would inevitably be a heavy, bulky structure, but by switching the concept to using lines and their tension, a lightweight structure becomes possible. I had a feeling that tensegrity would change the history of architecture.

For some reason, though, Fuller did not apply this tensegrity structure to his own geodesic dome. The structural system of his dome entailed supporting the dome with a frame, and filling the gaps in the frame with membranous

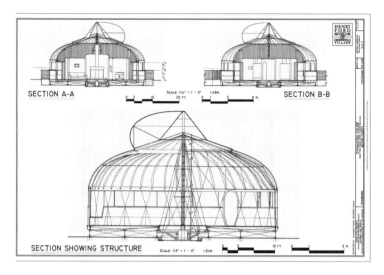

69 Dymaxion House. Historic American Buildings Survey.

material or glass, which play no role in supporting the structure. Even the brilliant Fuller could not escape from the frame principle.

Fuller was a philosopher who continually thought about how to move beyond the 20th century in every respect. In 1945 he launched the Dymaxion House,[69] which was a prefabricated domed house that could be built in a very short amount of time at extremely low cost (it was marketed as costing only $6,500). However, 20th-century Americans preferred traditional rectangular houses with old-fashioned decorative elements, and the company was quickly driven to bankruptcy.

It is almost as if Fuller were born too early. He had many dreams that transcended the 20th century, but his dreams were crushed under the weight of 20th-century technical limitations and popular tastes. The geodesic dome, while adhering to the prevailing mode of frame-oriented architecture, was simply not accepted in the 20th century.

We endeavoured to use Fuller's ideas to go further than Fuller did; to go beyond the frame orientation and 'Laugierism' of the geodesic dome. Whereas the standard tensegrity model employs rods (lines) as tensile members, our tensegrity dome derived its strength from the use of membranes (planes) as tensile members. This enabled us to exploit the potential of membranes as structural materials, rather than as materials that simply partition the interior and the exterior, which reduces the overall cost.

CELLS AND TENSEGRITY

The idea of tensegrity has also gained attention from the field of biology. In the 1970s, a cellular biologist named Donald E. Ingber (b. 1956) theorized that cells have tensegrity structures. When a cell is placed on a Petri dish, it is flattened and collapses, but Ingber noted that when he added an enzyme and removed it from the dish, a cell returned to a spherical shape. Ingber happened to learn about Fuller's tensegrity structure in a design class at Yale University, and hypothesized that the spherical structures of cells must result from tensegrity.

If we think of cells as mere balloons filled with a jelly-like substance, we cannot explain this phenomenon of re-expansion. However, hidden inside a cell is a three-dimensional network of protein fibres known as the cytoskeleton. The cells maintain their shape by utilizing the tension of this mesh. Each cell is attached to the substrate surrounding it at a point called a focal adhesion spot, so the dynamic environment outside the cell acts as a mechanism that transmits signals instantaneously through a network of protein fibres to every corner of the cell. This

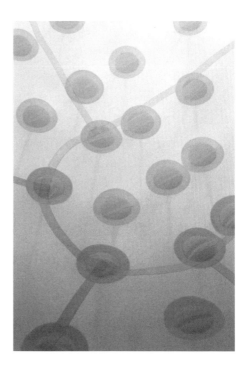

70 Inside Tee Haus. Adhesion parts between the polyester strings and the membrane that connects the double membranes.

mechanism is quite similar to the relationship between the membranes and the threads (lines) connecting the two membranes of the tea house we built in Frankfurt.[70]

Cells are not isolated points, but are interconnected through the tensile force of their planes and of the threads hidden within the planes, retaining their form, self-supporting and managing to survive in a world of overwhelming gravitational forces. It appears that Fuller's tensegrity, which he advocated as the structural system of the future, was already a basic principle of living organisms.

To return to Semper and Laugier, biology is moving towards a 'Semperian' understanding of organisms as networks of points, lines and planes that support the body, rather than a 'Laugierian' view, in which organisms are skeletons (frames). In this way, Fuller not only prophesied the future of architecture, but he also played a prophetic role in biology: through the agency of Ingber, Fuller's tensegrity brought about a paradigm shift in that field as well.

Back in Milan, the biggest difficulty with our 'Casa per Tutti' project turned out to be that we could not find a factory in Japan to make our specially shaped umbrellas. We eventually found Yoshihisa Iida, an artist who is known for his umbrella art. Iida handcrafts umbrellas of various shapes and sizes, and kindly took on our request for an umbrella with a zipper and extra triangular pieces of fabric. As Iida fabricates his umbrellas individually, it seemed groundbreaking for such a large structure to be based solely on the small-scale craft of umbrella making, but it was also a vulnerability, as we were wholly dependent on the hands of one person.

Thankfully, the umbrellas arrived just in time, and 15 students gathered on the green lawn of the Triennale venue in Milan to erect a pure white dome from interconnecting umbrellas with zippers. Once the structure was complete, a celebratory meal got underway, and the space inside was quite sufficient for 15 people. Covered with a white membrane, the interior was filled with soft white light, and without a bulky frame the supple fabric created a gentle, soothing atmosphere with a sense of security like an enfolding garment.

It is somewhat reassuring to think that no matter what kind of disaster occurs, if each person has one of these specially shaped umbrellas in their home, and brings it with them when evacuating, we will somehow be able to save ourselves. The wisdom of Semper, Fuller and the people of the Sahara Desert came together and bore fruit in Milan.

HOJO-AN, EIGHT CENTURIES ON

In 1212, the hermit Kamo no Chōmei (1115–1216) wrote one of his most famous works, *Hōjōki*, which is often translated as 'The Ten Foot Square Hut'. On the 800th anniversary of its writing, I unexpectedly received a request to design a 'contemporary Hojo-an' (the name of the hut in the book). The site was on the precincts of Shimogamo Shrine in Kyoto, where Kamo no Chōmei had lived.

Chōmei's life was marked by a series of personal tribulations in a turbulent time of wars, famines and natural disasters, and these gave rise to his philosophy and his view of architecture. In *Hōjōki*, Chōmei wrote: 'The flow of the river never ceases, and the water never stays the same. Bubbles float on the surface of pools, bursting, re-forming, never lingering. They're like the people in this world and their dwellings.

'In our bejewelled capital, fine buildings stand in rows, their gables competing for pre-eminence. The homes of the elite: one might think they're eternal, but ask around and you'll find, those with a long history are rare indeed. Great houses fade away, ultimately replaced by lesser ones. The same goes for people. The city and its crowds seem eternal, and yet, of the 20 or 30 people I knew long ago, only one or two are still around. They are like bubbles on the water, emerging at dusk and bursting before dawn.'

I have long been interested in *Hōjōki*'s principle that small, humble hovels are sublime, and what intrigues me most is the idea that Chōmei lived in a kind of mobile house. Not only did he see a small hut of about 3 m (10 feet) square as ideal, but his little dwelling was transportable on a cart. The logical conclusion of Chōmei's philosophy is to design the ultimate mobile house – small and portable – and this was the point of departure for the present-day Hojo-an project.

Ideas about how to proceed came from the theory that the walls of Chōmei's radical mobile dwelling were made of straw mats. While a wooden frame can be dismantled and piled on a cart, the same cannot be said of typical earthen walls. However, straw mats can easily be rolled up and placed on a cart, and they are light enough to be carried by hand. The idea that Chōmei lived in a hut made from a combination of wooden frames and straw mats, which he could easily transport, makes sense. In his own way, he must have skilfully combined lines and planes to create a mobile house, and I wondered if it was possible to create a contemporary version of his straw-mat house.

In place of straw mats, we settled on a new type of membranous material known as ETFE (ethylene fluoride ethylene copolymer). ETFE was originally developed for greenhouses, and was thought of as a cheap material for inexpensive and easily buildable structures such as greenhouses. However, because it is so light, strong, transparent and weather-resistant, it has recently been used for the roofs of huge buildings such as train stations, airports and sports stadiums.

The challenging issue was the structure that would support this membrane. It would be easy to build a wooden frame and wrap it with ETFE, but that would not be much of an update from Chōmei's time and the wooden frame would also be quite bulky. With eight centuries having passed, it was time for something new, so we began experimenting with a frameless structural system –

a Semper-style covered hut that would be suitable for a contemporary Hojo-an.

I drew inspiration from the structural system that supports the body of the sea cucumber, a squishy invertebrate that is also known for its firm flesh. Instead of a rigid skeleton, like that of fish and other vertebrates, the sea cucumber's endoskeleton consists of myriad microscopic bony fragments. The sea cucumber is therefore a master of tensegrity, making effective use of the tensile force of its skin and the compressive force of its bony fragments. This 'squishy but firm' structural system seems highly futuristic – light years ahead of the fusty old Laugierian frame structure.

For our Hojo-an we decided to use small, thin, seemingly weak wooden strips as the bony elements. Measuring just 20 × 30 mm (⅘ × 1 ⅕ in.), with a 20 mm (⅘ in.) square cross-sectional area, the idea was to attach these slender wooden rods (our 'bones') in a different array to each of three transparent ETFE sheets. Superimposing the three pieces with different bone patterns transformed the squishy planes (membranes) into something solid and firm, like a wall, but because they only had tiny pieces of wood embedded in them, each membrane could be rolled up like a straw mat and carried lightly under one's arm. Chōmei may have wandered around the half-ruined city with his straw mats just like that.

Another innovation was the use of powerful magnets to overlay the three pieces of ETFE, rather than metal bolts or adhesive. If bolts and adhesive are used, assembly and disassembly take time, but with magnets they can be carried out in an instant. By superimposing planes with magnets, we were able to create a mobile house that suddenly appears and disappears like a fog or haze.[71]

71 Hojo-an 2012 . Kyoto. Japan. Hojo-an's history dates back to 800 years ago. and it is often referred to as the prototype of miniature mobile houses in Japan. We regenerated the house for today using magnets and ETFE.

The idea for the powerful magnets came from Salvatore, the stonemason and owner of a Pietro Serena quarry in the mountains near Florence, Italy, who had been experimenting with powerful magnets to attach stone to walls. Traditionally, stone has been affixed to concrete walls using mortar or bolts, but this means the stone cannot easily be removed, and once in place, the construction is irreversible. However, magnets make it easy to install and uninstall stone without damaging it and Salvatore's idea was that when someone moves, they could simply remove the stone and reuse it in their new home. The idea of a portable interior is certainly intriguing, and somewhat similar to the Hojo-an model, but if the house itself is not light enough to be transportable by hand, then it cannot be called the 'Hojo-an of the future'.

The contemporary Hojo-an that appeared on the precincts of Shimogamo Shrine was so transparent and light, with such a faint presence, that one could easily have walked past it without noticing; it was as if thin strips of wood were floating in the Shimogamo Shrine forest. Looking as ephemeral as a mayfly, the structure was an architecture of planes (ETFE), points (powerful magnets at points of contact) and lines (arrays of wood strips as an endoskeleton) that resonate and reciprocally embed themselves, hovering around the body and protecting it. I am sure that even the cynical Chōmei would have been happy to observe this understated structure as he lurked in the shadows of the forest.

Eight hundred years after *Hōjōki*, times are again quite grim, and this is precisely why we must be prepared to start walking once more through this savage world carrying our flexible and friendly planes, the straw mats of today.

INDEX

Numerals in italic refer
to illustrations captions

PICTURE CREDITS

First published in Japan in 2020 in the Japanese language
under the title *Ten Sen Men* by Iwanami Shoten

First published in the United Kingdom in 2024 by
Thames & Hudson Ltd, 181A High Holborn,
London WC1V7QX

First published in the United States of America in 2024 by
Thames & Hudson Inc., 500 Fifth Avenue, New York,
New York 10110

Point Line Plane © Thames & Hudson Ltd
Text by Kengo Kuma © 2022 Kengo Kuma & Associates
Translated from the Japanese by Christopher Stephens
English language translation © 2024 Thames & Hudson
Ltd, London

Designed by Tom Etherington

British Library Cataloguing-in-Publication Data
A catalogue record for this book is available from
the British Library.

Library of Congress Control Number 2024932555

ISBN 978-0-500-02796-7

Printed in China by Toppan Leefung Printing Limited

MIX
Paper | Supporting
responsible forestry
FSC
www.fsc.org
FSC® C104723